I Want to Be a Youth Pastor

By Nancy Klassen

Dedicated to my Youth Pastor, Geoff
And to all my teenagers - I love you guys!

I Want to Be a Youth Pastor

© 2023 by Nancy Klassen

Cover Design by: Caitlin Herbert

ISBN: 979-8-218-16275-7

For Worldwide Distribution, Printed in the United States of America

www.nancyjolene.org

Contents

Acknowledgements 5

Preface 7

Introduction 9

Chapter 1 – The Beginning 13

Chapter 2 – The Teenagers 19

Chapter 3 – The Volunteers 31

Chapter 4 – The Parents 41

Chapter 5 – The Games & Snacks 51

Chapter 6 – The Studying & Teaching 59

Chapter 7 – The Counseling 67

Chapter 8 – LGBTQ 77

Chapter 9 – Suicide 87

Chapter 10 – How to Hear God 97

Chapter 11 – Prayer 109

Chapter 12 – Other Tips 121

Chapter 13 – Transition Time 135

Chapter 14 – Your Life as a Youth Pastor 143

Chapter 15 – The Greatest Moments 155

Testimonies 161

Acknowledgements

Mike and Sherry, words cannot express my appreciation and gratitude for you both. Our divine connection in 2009 was of God and I will forever be grateful for all the years of ministry guidance you have given me. This book contains so much of what I learned from you and I know it will help many others in ministry. Thank you for letting me have the chance to start the youth group and lead those kids! It was both a privilege and an honor to serve alongside you in the ministry during the time we had together. To God be the glory!

To all the volunteers and leaders throughout the years who helped with the youth group, (you know who you are!) thank you from the bottom of my heart. I know many teenagers were blessed to know you, be around you, and learn from your wisdom. Thank you for working with me and being gracious with my mistakes. I learned so much from being around you. We all grew together and I so appreciate your help in every area you served. Thank you!

Jodee, Caitlin, Velvet, and Mark, thank you so much for all your help in the formatting, editing, and designing process of this book! You guys have all been such a blessing to me, I could not have done this without you, thank you!

To my family and friends, thank you for all your support and encouragement during the writing process. What a project this has been! Your ideas and advice were so helpful and I am very excited to finally be able to share this with you!

6

Preface

Teenagers. I love them. Most are just hungry for love and attention—they want to feel like they are a part of something; they want to belong. They are full of quirks, comments, and the unexpected. Getting through this awkward, youthful stage of life is never without its struggles, but these incredibly formative years can be filled with the goodness of God and teenagers need to know it! Jesus desires for everyone on this planet to be in relationship with Him and finding Him in the teenage years is so much better than later on in life, when too many life lessons are learned the hard way.

There isn't a need to talk about the generation that is growing up before our eyes. Single-parent homes doing their best, families full of strife, schools filled with violence, massive social media influence all converging in a time where a screen brings more comfort than a human. When we look too long at the issues at hand, it can seem like an insurmountable problem that will never be fixed, but the harvest is ready! We are laborers for the Lord, and our part is to lift up our eyes to where our Help comes from. He is mighty, and He is able!

This book was born out of the time I had with my teenagers while I was their youth pastor. God's call on my life to pastor was revealed as I took the step in starting the youth ministry at my church in Wyoming. My passion to minister to teenagers came from the positive experience I had growing up attending my youth group, the need for a youth ministry at my church, and because of who my youth pastor was to me—a caring, genuine, and really fun guy who made Jesus real to me.

You may have just graduated Bible College and are in search of a ministry position. You may have a teaching gift that you want to exercise, or you may feel the Lord nudging you to serve in this area at your church. Whatever the case may be, a genuine love for junior high and high school students is the number one must-have. Love has always been the answer—God's kind of love. Unconditional, patient, and willing to look past faults and wrongs. It seems rare these days to find that kind of love operating in someone but you can always tell when it's the real thing. Teenagers are looking for the real thing.

What I share in the following pages is not the ultimate guide to youth ministry. There is no formula and your youth group will look different than mine, but I want to share some things I have learned that I believe will encourage you as you lead your own group of teenagers. I don't claim to have all the answers and you will most likely see things from a different perspective! God made us all different on purpose and as we work together, we can accomplish His will in the earth. Take what you can from what you read in this book and pass it on to others. Give Him all the glory, all the honor, and all the praise!

*My teenage years were without a cell phone. A few of my friends had their own phone, but it was just beginning to be normal when I graduated high school. The world has changed drastically in this area which has affected how youth ministry operates and functions.

Introduction

My youth group as a teenager was awesome. Like any pre-teen, I couldn't wait to be in seventh grade so I could finally go to youth group, have fun with my friends, and be around the older kids! They were so cool, and I wanted to be one of them. Our small town of 1500 people had a community-wide youth group that met at one of the churches. Every Tuesday, we would walk from school to the church, drop our backpacks when we came through the doors, and run to the fellowship hall where snacks awaited. Our youth pastor was there to welcome us and ask us about our day, and soon we were all having a great time laughing and telling stories.

Game time came after filling up on chips or donuts. We would often play dodge ball, capture the flag, or some other type of game that involved running around or throwing things. The guys made sure to get out the hockey sticks to challenge our youth pastor, Geoff, to some floor hockey, while us girls watched and shared the details of our day. Of course, we would often talk about which guy was the best looking or who had a crush on who. Geoff would frequently run over and lean on the counter to hear all the gushy details while the boys kept playing. We would all giggle and turn red when he guessed right. He would laugh, promise not to tell, then head back to the game. When the boys weren't looking, he would casually glance at us making secret gestures to which boy one of the girls liked. Even as I write this, it makes me smile thinking back on those days.

Next up was Bible Study downstairs where you raced to get a good spot on a couch—or a pillow for the floor at the very least. Seventh and eighth graders went straight to Bible

9

Study, but high schoolers spent time in worship before Bible Study began. A few songs were picked, and two or three teenagers would sing, while another played the guitar. Then, Pastor Geoff would get out the black music stand, open his Bible, and teach a message that challenged us to discover who God was and what the Christian life looked like for a believer. He would close the night with prayer, and then it was hang-out time until our parents picked us up or we finally had the privilege to drive ourselves home.

Fridays were fun nights. Activities were planned for the upcoming month, and the letter in the mail with the details inside always hung on the fridge at home. Snail mail—what a relic! Camping trips, girls/guys nights, progressive suppers, competitions, fundraisers, dinner theatres, movie nights, you name it, we most likely did it! Certain events were annual like the Valentine's banquet, the Christmas party, or a Youth Sunday church service etc. Every four years, our group raised the money to fly to Mexico during spring break to build a house for a family and to help at an orphanage. There was always something to look forward to, and nobody wanted to miss an event.

Of course, as with any group of people (and especially a group of teenagers) it wasn't perfect. Somebody wouldn't play by the rules in a game, friendships were ruffled, parents were called, someone would get made fun of—it wasn't always smooth sailing. Not everyone is always going to get along when you bring a big group together but you can come pretty close! It was a great youth group to be in and God was at the heart of it all helping us grow and change to become more like Him.

I have often reflected on that time as such a highlight in my life. It was so much fun to hang out with that group of people every week, and I always looked forward to going. Every moment that happened in that church building helped me grow as an individual and as a believer in Jesus. It was a place of safety and security where we learned to be bold and pray out loud in front of everyone, where we shared what we were going through, where we helped each other and made lasting friendships. Those moments are never wasted, and I am so thankful we had such a great youth pastor to lead us in that season of our lives.

As a teenager, you don't realize all the preparation, dedication, and faithfulness it takes to have a youth ministry. All you care about is having fun and being around your friends! But Geoff and his wife, along with several volunteers, made it all happen, and they were dedicated to the goal of reaching as many teenagers as possible with the love of Jesus. I imagine the amount of time spent planning and organizing each event was no small task, but it always came together and was a success in my mind. What a blessing it was to have leaders wanting to make a difference and using their talents and gifts to serve the Lord!

I don't recall if there was a specific thing Geoff said, a teaching that stands out, a biblical truth that changed my course in life, or our cool, secret handshake (haha). But I will say this—it was who Geoff was that made the most impact on me. I watched him say hi to everyone and show genuine interest in how their life was going. I will always remember his kindness, his goofy laugh, and I knew I could ask him anything and he did his best to share what he felt God wanted me to hear. He yielded to the Holy Spirit and let God use him, and you could see he loved the Lord with all his heart. The compassion of Jesus shined through Geoff week after week to every teenager that came through those church doors, and year after year he was faithful to be what God called him to be—a youth pastor.

Even as a teenager, I remember thinking that if I were ever in charge of a youth group, I would want to be just like Geoff. The opportunity arose sooner than I thought as I found myself packing my suitcase and heading off into my very first adventure with God—Wyoming!

Chapter 1

The Beginning

In 2009, a divine connection made with a pastor and his wife brought me to their ministry in Wyoming following my high school graduation. At the time, I had no idea it was God's leading—I just wanted to do what God wanted me to do and living in the States sounded like a fun adventure! At that point in my life, I was very unsure of how to hear His voice, but I took a step of faith and said yes to coming. Looking back now, He definitely directed every step of the way. I graduated in Canada, and within a few months I was down in America experiencing another country, a different culture, and attending a new home church.

Each night my church had a service I would watch the teenagers coming through the doors, and all the memories I had of my youth group would float to the forefront of my mind. All I could think of was how they needed a youth group like how I had back home. As my church became home to me, I began to entertain the idea of what a youth ministry could look like and what it would all entail. A call I did not know I had on the inside of me by God Himself became a passion I wanted to see come to fruition in that church body.

After living in the States for a few years, I asked my pastor if I could start the youth group for our church. I was very happy to receive the go-ahead and thanked God for the opportunity that had been given to me. By that time, a good foundation in the Word had been laid. I had been a sponge soaking in all the teachings from my pastor, and I was learning how to walk by faith in my own personal life. I had been faithfully involved in the ministry and had gained a few years of experience team teaching the younger kids with the associate pastor of our church. My relationship with God was flourishing, and I had begun to personally hear Him and recognize His voice. So much growth happened in such a short amount of time, but all of it prepared me for taking the step of faith to lead my own youth group.

Under my pastor's direction to have both male and female leadership, I asked one of my single guy friends if he wanted to help me. He was all for it! We shared the same heart for the kids and made a great team immediately. I can remember the excitement we shared for what our youth group would look like and how much fun we would have! We wanted our group to be welcoming, a place where each teenager could feel safe to share what they were going through, and, in turn, we could offer biblical help and guidance from the Word. I wanted those kids to know God and be able to hear Him, and sharing the weight of leading a youth group with my friend meant so much to me.

There were several youth groups in my town already, so I went around and introduced myself to several of the youth pastors in the area. I figured I could gain some wisdom from those who had gone before me, and they were wonderful to meet and get to know! We all wanted the teenagers in our town to know Jesus, regardless of our denominational affiliation. In later years, we would even plan joint youth events in the summer. What a joy it is to work in unity with believers of other church bodies! After all, we are Christians, and we are all on the same team.

The first night of youth group was thrilling, and I could hardly wait to meet the teenagers that were going to come!

But, right off the bat I missed it. I tried to pattern this new youth group exactly after the youth group I grew up attending—even down to the day of the week we met. I had decided since my hometown youth group was successful meeting on Friday nights, then it would make sense in Wyoming, right? Wrong. I announced the new youth group would meet every other Friday evening, and, sure enough, those Friday nights were slow-going for a long time. A full night meant at least three teens showed up. What I had to realize was that the already-designated youth group night in the area was Wednesday night. After-school programs and sports were not scheduled on Wednesdays for that very reason. When we adjusted our youth night to the mid-week meeting, we had more teens start to come in.

During those first few weeks, and especially into that first year, there were changes that needed to be made. What we often planned didn't turn out how we thought it would, but quick and easy changes brought a more fluid movement. Certain activities took more or less time than estimated, discipline needed to be enforced, and we were quickly finding out how to walk in our leadership roles. Overall, we kept our teenagers the priority and interacted with them as much as possible for the few short hours we had them.

For a long time, we had only a handful of teenagers show up—no more than four or five. We were just happy that they came! I learned very quickly how much teaching they could handle, and where they were at with God. In the beginning, we just had kids from our church, so we already knew them pretty well and didn't need a lot of ice breaking to make them feel comfortable. As the group increased in size over the years, more kids came that had never been to church and didn't know much about God at all. It seemed like the Lord brought the increase as we were able to handle it.

We shared with the kids what we wanted our group to look like fairly early on. We always emphasized that every teenager was welcome to come no matter what they looked like or what they were into. We wanted the churched and unchurched, the Christian and the non-Christian, the teens who drank, the ones who smoked, the girls who were pregnant, the ones with an addiction, anyone that looked different—we wanted them all to come, and we told our kids to invite them! "For the Son of man has come to seek and to save that which was lost" (Luke 19:10, *NKJV*). Everyone deserves the chance to know about Jesus.

The simple format of snacks, games, worship, then Bible Study became our Wednesday night rhythm that lasted many years. We would eat pizza and brownies, play games outside, then head in for the worship portion of the night. A few songs were played on guitar or on the screens at the front of the church while we all sang. The message from God was shared, questions were answered, and I would pray to close out the night. Those few hours always went by so fast and before you knew it the night was over.

There was always a window of time to minister personally to some of them before they left. I had some teenagers that would come right up and want prayer while others would linger in the background deciding if they were brave enough to tell a leader what was going on in their life. Most would make a beeline for the last of the snacks and head out the doors but many, many kids throughout the years were touched by God during and after a message. The Holy Spirit would minister to those kids exactly what they needed, and He affected their lives in such a beautiful way. This was always my favorite part of the night. I loved watching them being set free by God.

As I processed how the night went on my drive home, I would sometimes wonder if I was doing a good enough job. Other nights, I would be ecstatic because it went so well and would thank God all the way home for what He called me to! You simply cannot rely on your feelings—you just do what God asks you to do. "For we walk by faith, not by sight" (2 Cor. 5:7, *KJV*). At my pastors' request, I would either text or call them to share the details of the night. Sometimes, they would ask me to adjust how I did something, but most of the time they just wanted to hear the good things that were going on. I often used that time to ask them questions or gain some wisdom in knowing what to do for future events.

As I reflected upon each youth night, there were parts of leading a youth group that I really wondered about. Was this my calling or was this just temporary? Could I teach them well and minister effectively for the Kingdom? Personally, I had lived a pretty clean life during my teenage years. I never drank, used drugs, or went to parties. I never even dated in high school. I was the classic good Christian kid, and because of my upbringing, I wondered if I would even be able to help teenagers with some of the issues they were facing. Thankfully, you don't have to go through bad things to help someone. It may give you a better angle at how to minister, and you will understand a lot better where they are coming from, but it's not required. And it's not about you. The Word is what heals and makes people clean (John 15:3), you just have to sow the Word.

Looking back now, I appreciate those first days of youth group with those four to five kids that would come. It was a great start in learning the role of youth pastor, and I learned a lot from them. As our group began to grow throughout the years, it was awesome to watch more teens come through the doors and know God for the first time! As other team members joined, more kids were reached with the gospel and fruit began to show. It was wonderful to see. There were moments I would look around the room watching interactions take place—friendships being formed, laughter around a table, a team leader praying with a teenager—it all made me smile and think, "I'm so glad God picked me to do this!"

When my friend and I started that youth group, I had no idea that I would be youth pastoring for almost nine years. I didn't even know at the time that I was called by God into the fivefold ministry. I just wanted a place for teenagers to learn who Jesus was and found myself coming to the realization that He had indeed placed the call on my life to pastor. What an amazing chapter it turned out to be! There were many challenges and many victories—so much to grow in and learn. But God was so faithful through it all. He taught me much during those years, and I loved my kids. You will, too.

The following pages contain the many experiences I had while I served as the youth pastor for my church in Wyoming. I'm also going to share with you some wisdom I learned along the way. If you are just starting out or already in the middle of pastoring or helping with a youth ministry, I hope this book will be a great tool for you! Always remember, your time with your teenagers is a treasure and a gift. God has given you the honor and privilege of raising up young disciples for Him. Shepherd them well and be the best example of Jesus you can be. He is so pleased when we answer His call.

Chapter 2

The Teenagers

You will meet every type of personality known to man in a youth group. I can't begin to describe how interesting and hilarious this will be. Some will mesh really well with your personality, others not as much, but they will all become so special to you and a real joy to be around. The grace to love each teenager is there if you tap into it. The love of God toward these kids will come through you, and they pick up pretty quickly if you truly care about them or not. The temptation can come to look at the negative traits of the kids, so be watchful of that and do your best to not fall into the ditch of playing favorites (Rom. 2:11). Find at least one thing you like about each teenager and focus your attention on that. Enjoy them for their uniqueness. They are deep in a season of finding out who they are, and God is so pleased with each one.

Every youth group seems to have the same typical personality stereotypes but they all bring something unique to the group. You will get the kids that are super popular among their peers as well as the teenagers that are totally fine being in the background, not getting noticed. There will be ones that are there to just have a good time and others that had to talk themselves into coming for the first time, palms sweaty from being nervous at the unknown. These characteristics provide quite the variety for a youth group, and God designed it that way! He delights in our differences; it's what pulls us together and keeps us strong. It is His order, His way, and we are His delight.

There is a common ground that all teenagers share: each one wants to belong and feel accepted. Each one has a heart cry to fill that empty space on the inside. Each one wants to be whole and happy and fulfilled. We, as youth pastors, need to look beneath the surface of these teenagers. Under that exterior is the real them, a spirit being with the life that God breathed in. How can we best shepherd them? Do they know they are God's dearly loved? Do they believe there is a purpose and a plan for their life (Jer. 29:11)? What can we do to show them the love of God in a tangible way? As you navigate the journey of being their youth pastor, always come back to the simplicity of what is truly needed: just Jesus.

What teenagers need is an encounter with God. Their eyes tell a story. I see the teenage girl who has never had the affirmation from her dad that she's beautiful and worth waiting for. I see her showing more skin and wearing tighter clothes to attract a guy to fill the part of her that's been left wanting. I see the teenage guy who struggles with porn, who wants to feel like a man, but doesn't know how to get there. I see him trying to prove himself and show everyone he's not a failure. I see the cut marks on arms where they took a blade to their skin to stop the pain inside. I see behind the layers of makeup covering what they don't want seen. It's in their eyes. There's joy and light, or emptiness and longing. Am I enough? Was I a mistake? Do I matter? Am I loved? All of their questions and insecurities will melt away in His presence. One encounter with God erases doubt and fear and lack of any kind. To know He understands is a gift from heaven (Heb. 4:15-16).

I have watched kids have miraculous encounters with God on a youth night. He touches their hearts so deeply, and you can see them trying to process what happened. One word from heaven answers all their inner confusion. When they know they are loved just as they are, and not for what they do, it brings freedom, and their chains of bondage are broken. Depression, suicide, feelings of unworthiness, guilt, and self-harm get washed away under the blood of Jesus that rushes through them, leaving them free and cleansed. "He saved us, not because of works done by us in righteousness, but according to His own mercy, by the washing of regeneration and renewal of the Holy Spirit, whom He poured out on us richly through Jesus Christ our Savior" (Titus 3:5-6, *ESV*). It is no accident they showed up to your youth group—there is purpose in them being there, and God loves to show up big time for His teenagers.

As the Lord reaches these kids week after week, begin to develop relationships with them yourself. Ask them about their favorite everything and make mental notes about the things they like. Show them you truly care and that they matter. Tease them, laugh with them, enjoy them! They will become more comfortable around you, and when they feel safe with you—and when trust has been built—they will open up and share about their lives. As that door opens, you will be able to channel the wisdom and life of God into them and watch their lives increase in ways they never thought possible. God is all about relationship, and we should be, too.

When you look beneath the surface at these God-given personalities, you will learn that you can't put your teenagers in a box, especially when they are going through a hard time. You will have one that might never say a word about it and be crying on their bed every night trying to process what's happening. Another might send you a text in the middle of the night hinting that they are having trouble, but not wanting anyone else to know. Still another will pull you aside and tell you every detail in private, desperate to know how to handle what's going on. All three of these actions can come from one personality type. You just can't put your teens into a category with a label and think they will always react and respond in a certain way. Be open and unassuming, and believe the best of everyone.

Your kids will come from blended families, single-parent homes, foster care, homeless shelters, and every type of background. You will get the teens that only have one parent and are missing the other, wondering if it's their fault that their parent isn't around. You will get ones that absolutely despise their parents and just want a home without the yelling and screaming. They plan their escapes, they think about how to make it on their own, they vow on the inside they will never again live like they do. Some teenagers raise themselves and couch surf at friends' houses because of parents that are never around. It seems rare these days for a teenager to come from a solid home with two parents who love each other, so in a way, youth group might become the family some of your kids have never had. "God sets the solitary in families; He brings out those who are bound…" (Psalm 68:6, *NKJV*). You, as their youth pastor, have the privilege of introducing them into the greatest family they will ever be a part of with God as their Father who will be the one to never leave them. "…for He has said, "I will never leave you nor forsake you" (Heb. 13:5, *ESV*).

You will have both Christian and non-Christian kids in your youth group. Most of the kids who have grown up in Christian homes are riding off the coattails of their parents' faith, which is a fairly normal thing to do. Eventually the realization comes that they need a relationship with Jesus for themselves apart from their parents. The group you are working with is right around the age of deciding if they really want God or not. It's a time where you have a lot of fence-sitters, and kids deciding if they want to go the world's way or go with God. Keep the simplicity of Christ ever present; salvation and relationship are gifts to be received, not worked for. "But as many as received Him, to them He gave the right to become children of God, to those who believe in His name" (John 1:12, *NKJV*). Just keep answering their questions and pointing them to Jesus. You can't make them choose God, so don't be pushy, but let each decide for themselves.

Some of your teens will be more advanced and show greater maturity than their peers, but not all of them will reach that stage as quickly as you might think. There will be some teens who cling to you and follow you around, which can be challenging when you have many other kids that need ministered to. "Take heed that you do not despise one of these little ones, for I say to you that in heaven their angels always see the face of My Father who is in heaven. For the Son of Man has come to save that which was lost" (Matt. 18:10-11, *NKJV*). Find a time when they aren't around you, and then purposely seek them out to show them that they are valuable and that you see them. It's also important to just be real with your teenagers. Don't treat them like they are immature and don't know anything. Talk to them just like you would talk to an adult. They can handle it, and they respond better when you do.

There is a strong possibility of having a pastor's kid in your youth group. Treat them no differently than any other person in the room "For there is no respect of persons with God" (Rom. 2:11, *KJV*). They need grace for mistakes just like everyone else. They often feel an expectation to be perfect and can get into fear over making a wrong choice. Pastors' kids could also end up on the other side of the ditch trying to be rebellious pushing every boundary possible. If you have this teenager in your group through their four years of high school, there is a possibility of seeing both extremes in the same person. This is not always the case, but watch that you don't put unnecessary expectations on them. They need affirmation that their identity is not in the position their parents hold, but in Jesus. Also, just because they are a son or daughter of a pastor does not mean that God has called them to be in the fivefold ministry as well. Put no undue pressure on them. Let them find out who they are in Christ, just like every other teenager in your youth group.

It boggles my mind that certain kids can party all week long and be doing who knows what, but then make it to youth group every Wednesday without fail. They are so often starving on the inside for God and know they need help, but they struggle trying to break the habits of the flesh on their own. In Matthew 18:12-14, Jesus describes people as sheep who are led astray, and Himself as the Good Shepherd who always comes to find them—even if there is only one missing out of one hundred others. How awesome it is that we are the ones that Jesus left the ninety-nine for and that we mean everything to Him! Your teens may cause a bit of trouble now and then, and you might have to frequently check that they aren't getting into anything they shouldn't, but your kids are soft on the inside of that rough exterior and in need of love. Never condemn them for their mistakes. That isn't your job. The transformation that is needed will happen when they turn to the Lord, and it is amazing to watch (2 Cor. 5:17). You may not see it for years but seeds of life are being planted in them while they are sitting in a chair listening to you week after week.

Certain kids can be overlooked because on the outside they seem stable and level-headed. You will assume they are just fine because they are doing well in school, they may attend church regularly, and they come from a decent home. This doesn't mean that they are 100% fine on the inside. Each teenager has a season where they need help. Some of these kids have told me they didn't want to say anything about having trouble because they knew others had it worse than them. They didn't want to be a bother with their little problem. It may be easier to pay more attention to the teens with the bigger issues because they are more noticeable, but ask God to help you see from His viewpoint. He sees the ones that never say anything, and they may need just as much help as those other kids. Reassure them that their problem is not nothing. God cares about every detail of their lives. Even "the very hairs of your head are all numbered" (Luke 12:7, *NKJV*). We are all of great value to Him.

When a teen breaks down in tears right in front of you, hug them, and love them, and hear what's on the inside of their heart. Sometimes, you don't need to say anything. It doesn't matter what the situation was or if it's valid that they are crying. What matters is Jesus came "to heal the brokenhearted" (Luke 4:18, *NKJV*), and He might just need you to show them His love through a simple hug. Do you see why we cannot walk out our role as youth pastor without the Holy Spirit? There is no way in the natural to know exactly how to handle each personality, issue, and solve every problem in our own understanding. We are not the Holy Spirit. "If any of you lacks wisdom, let him ask God, who gives generously to all without reproach, and it will be given him" (Jas. 1:5, *ESV*). We need Him. For everything.

Remaining "calm and cool and steady" (2 Tim. 4:5, *AMP*) before your kids matters. Teenage emotions can be quite the rollercoaster ride, but when they see stability, it brings a sense of safety to many teens who don't get to be around safety very often. God will help you to be sure and steady around them like how He is for you. They will sense the peace you have in Jesus and how He lives through you in the way you conduct yourself. You may be the only example of Jesus they will see for a long time, so "let your light so shine before men, that they may see your good works, and glorify your Father which is in heaven" (Matt. 5:16, *KJV*). What levels out these emotions from the soul realm is coming into His presence and letting Him wipe the tears away while He stills the anxious thoughts. As you welcome the Holy Spirit into your night with the kids, His presence will calm their fears and hold them steady.

One of my favorite things about being around teenagers is seeing what God has put on the inside of them. They have talents and giftings lying dormant just waiting to be discovered. God has placed such massive potential in each of them just waiting to be released when the time is right. When they discover something that gives them purpose and opens up a door into their future, it's like watching a flower bloom for the first time. Get excited with them when they become stirred up at seeing the possibilities of who they can become. Encourage them to find that path the Lord wants for them! There is no greater fulfillment than doing what the Lord calls us to do.

Keep an eye out for teenagers who may be called into the ministry. "And He gave some apostles, and some prophets, and some evangelists, and some pastors and teachers; for the perfecting of the saints, for the work of the ministry, for the edifying of the body of Christ" (Eph. 4:11-12, *KJV*). God may or may not show you which ones they are. If He shows you, He may not want you to say anything to them. Their gifting and call may be clear to you, but it's good for them to hear from God for themselves. A few of my teens throughout the years came to me privately wondering if ministry might be in their future. When they begin to see what the Lord wants them to do, it's an awesome opportunity to speak into their life. You may be able to help them be more spiritually prepared for what is ahead. Share some wisdom you have learned if they ask and pray with them about the steps in their future. Have them help you with a few things in the church so they gain some experience and get their feet wet in the water of ministry life. No preparation time is ever wasted.

The Word tells us not to be childish, but to remain childlike in faith. Your teenagers are coming out of their childish adolescent stage and developing into strong young men and women of God. They will be sponges most of the time, soaking up much of what you say and teach. They have not had decades of life experience, or built unnecessary layers and walls around them. Most are so teachable and open to the things of God, so fill them up with His goodness and pour in solid truth so they begin to stand on a firm foundation. "For no other foundation can anyone lay than that which is laid, which is Jesus Christ" (1 Cor. 3:11, *NKJV*). Much of their character development is formed in their earlier years, so make the most of it. My prayer was that enough foundation would be laid in the Word of righteousness during their high school years that they would know how to hold fast to their King with that childlike faith when they left home.

Some kids will learn and grow faster than the others. You cannot put them on a scale and expect them all to move at the same pace. You will have some spiritual babies in your youth group the entire time they are there from seventh grade all the way to senior year. You will also have seventh graders come in who may grow so much in the Lord you will be blown away by their spiritual maturity by the time they graduate. Everyone takes time to grow in all areas and all stages; you cannot hurry them. Some are slow and steady, and some are sprinters, but you can encourage all of them to move forward in their life race. "...let us also lay aside every weight, and the sin which so easily ensnares us, and let us run with endurance the race that is set before us, looking unto Jesus, the author and finisher of our faith..." (Heb. 12: 1-2, *NKJV*).

When your teenagers make Jesus their own and go to God first instead of you, they have crossed a major threshold toward maintaining a close relationship with God throughout their life. It's exciting to hear them talk about their own personal relationship with God developing and how He is showing up for them! When you see their eyes light up because they realize Jesus is theirs, nothing compares to that joy. For some this comes early on, and for others you may not get to see it in the time you have them, but this is what shepherding is all about—leading and caring for them along their journey until they see the Great Shepherd for themselves and begin to have Him as their Number One.

Your role as a youth pastor is much more important than you think. Sure, you may be mowing the church yard, clipping the hedges, taking out the trash, and scrubbing toilets during the week, but the call on the inside will never remain quiet. It will always be part of you and it will surface often. I don't know who's going to read this book, but I'm going to guess that some of you out there have quit pastoring because you got hurt. But I'm telling you right now, God needs you back in. Lives depend on it. Souls are aching to know Christ as their Savior. "The harvest truly is plenteous, but the laborers are few" (Matt. 9:37, *KJV*). Teenagers are crying out for justice and oppression to be lifted. We must forgive and we must "press toward the mark for the prize of the high calling of God in Christ Jesus" (Phil. 3:13-14, *KJV*).

Maybe you haven't been in His presence for a long time. I'm asking Jesus to meet you now in the room where you are to heal your wounds, dry your tears, and show you His deep love for you. One of my favorite verses that has come to mean so much to me in the more difficult moments is Psalm 23:3, "He restores my soul" (*NKJV*). The soul is your mind, your will, and your emotions. Allow Him to minister to you in the places where you have been hurt. Receive your healing touch from Jesus today.

~

God, we ask for Your wisdom. Help us breathe life into these teenagers with your Word, and make us vessels before your feet. Heal us in the areas where we have been wounded. Take us to your very throne room for the grace we need to live out each day. Help us be servants of the King as we carry out the will of the Father through the words we speak and the lives we touch for Your glory. In Jesus' Name.

Chapter 3

The Volunteers

Unless your youth group is small, you will most likely be working with several different volunteers. Having a team of support around you is incredibly beneficial for any type of ministry. Volunteers that come to serve bring their own unique giftings, talents, and ideas. You cannot do it all, and they are there to help and aid you in leading the group of kids that are in your charge. Don't overuse anyone or burn them out—they have lives, too. You may get to choose your volunteers, or they may be assigned and already in place. However they come, they need to be appreciated and feel like they are a part of the team. Be generous in saying thank you. They are giving their time, attention, and their heart for the teens, and what a blessing it is to share with them the vision that God has given for your group.

The number of volunteers needed can be a bit tricky. I found that it worked well to have one youth leader per four to five teenagers. If there are too many leaders, the kids will be overwhelmed, shy away, and not speak up as much. If there aren't enough leaders, it can get out of control, and it's hard to keep an eye on that many at once. Some of the kids will connect with another youth leader more than you, which is 100% okay. They don't all have to come to you for everything. Take the advice of Jethro and what he shared with his son-in-law, Moses, in the eighteenth chapter of Exodus. Don't wear yourself out. Divide what you can among the people that have joined your team so you aren't doing all the work. When your leaders share the responsibility, it will help them develop their own gifting from God and allow you to focus more specifically on what God needs you to be doing.

Some volunteers will be there to learn alongside the kids themselves, which is awesome! Youth group is a great spot to grow spiritually, especially for new believers, leaders, or teenagers. Bringing in some hands-on help to prep for events and activities is needed, but until those volunteers are more comfortable with ministering themselves, let them soak in the preached Word during Bible Study time. Get an idea of where they are spiritually so you don't put them in a leadership or teaching position too quickly. The book of 1 Timothy will help in this area. Invest some extra time in them, if you can, and grow them up quickly because there is always a need for good leadership.

Some of your adult team members will bring the wisdom of many years. Learn from their past experiences, and gain insight by listening to what they choose to share with you. You will save a lot of time and energy in certain areas if you are open to hearing what they have to say. On the other hand, remember, you are the youth pastor, and they are serving under your leadership. Don't get intimidated by them when they are older than you. "Let no one despise your youth, but be an example to the believers in word, in conduct, in love, in spirit, in faith, in purity" (1 Tim. 4:12, *NKJV*). Submission to leadership is a biblical principle that goes for any age. "Obey your spiritual leaders and do what they say. Their work is to watch over your souls, and they are accountable to God" (Heb. 13:17, *NLT*). Likewise, don't treat your younger team members with contempt or demand submission and loyalty. Be a good leader by being a good example. Have a servant's heart while "submitting yourselves one to another in the fear of God" (Eph. 5:21, *KJV*).

Any group united brings a strong platform for the Gospel to be preached. "Behold, how good and pleasant it is when brothers dwell in unity" (Psa. 133:1, *ESV*)! Regardless of the age or what stage of life your volunteers are in, each will bring something valuable to your youth group, and you will all help each other come up higher in many ways. I find that the young volunteers bring fresh ideas and understand a bit better what the teenagers are going through since they are not far apart in age. The married volunteers often bring a needed authority and disciplined balance to the group. The single volunteers bring energy, flexibility, and are usually able to help a bit more and stay later. The older volunteers bring a calm and steady faithfulness that is a great comfort. Both male and female volunteers are awesome examples for the whole group of teens. You will all learn from each other in many ways as you work together.

The opposite personalities on your team will grow and challenge you, which is a good thing. Do not look down upon your "sandpaper person," and do not ignore them or avoid communication with them. God often puts two very different people together because of how it will strengthen both. "Iron sharpens iron, so a man sharpens the countenance of his friend" (Prov. 27:17, *NKJV*). Each volunteer brings value. Make room. Let the Holy Ghost have room. There will probably be times of contention and frustration you will have to walk through with the grace and help of the Holy Spirit. Do your best to understand where they are coming from, and realize your way isn't always the best way. What they bring to the table is often the answer you were searching for in the first place. Pray with them, listen to their ideas, and say thank you. You're a team.

"Write the vision and make it plain on tablets, that he may run who reads it" (Hab. 2:2, *NKJV*). Hear from God, write down the vision for your youth group, then share it with your team. Always tell them any new endeavors that will be implemented before announcing them to your youth kids. Pull the volunteers aside after Bible Study for a team meeting, or, if you have a weekly get together, use that time to share what's going to happen next. You are showing them they are a valuable part and are appreciated. Give them a chance to share their ideas or what they may have heard from God as well! It's also a great time to pray and lay things before the Lord to see what He wants. United in vision and prayer, you will take great ground for the Kingdom.

Not all volunteers are called to be helping you and your youth group. Submit to and keep in alignment with your lead pastors and what they ask of you but be wise to people who want to serve. You as youth pastor are a shepherd, and protection of the flock is important (Acts 20:28-30). Many people just aren't a good fit for ministering to teenagers, and that is okay! Pray for the right people to be in the right place at the right time doing the right thing. Where is their heart? Some may come with wrong motives, some aren't ready for it, some will show up because they feel obligated, but this all goes back to being led by the Holy Spirit. God obviously can work a lot of good in situations like these, but you will save time, energy, and unnecessary weight by prayerfully opening up the door for people who are supposed to be in leadership.

In addition to regular teaching, small group time is also beneficial. Teenagers will be open to sharing a lot more in a small group of four or five people versus speaking in front of everyone else. Train your team how to facilitate and lead small discussion groups so you are able to have more in-depth sharing time with the kids. You and your volunteers obviously don't have to know all the answers to the questions that will be asked, but discussion time is a great way to learn what's going on in a teenager's life and connect on a deeper level. Have your teams listen to what they are dealing with, pray with the kids, and offer biblical counsel. If they are nervous and intimated by the kids, encourage them! They will become more comfortable as they spend more time in their leadership role.

When the last teenager has left the building on a youth night, clean-up time should come next and a quick recap with your leaders about what all went on that evening. Depending on how many kids were there, each leader probably had different conversations with different kids and taken care of situations that the others didn't see. Talk about any red flags you saw and answer any questions they may have about what went on that night. It's a good idea to pray right there as a group for any kids that are really struggling, and pray for each other as well. You can take care of many traps the devil tries to set by simply taking this time to talk and pray with each other. Keep the communication lines open, and resolve any type of conflict or confusion between you and your leaders as quickly as possible. Stand with your team and thank God for a wonderful night.

Establish honor and work with excellence alongside the people you are serving with. Treat them well (Matt. 7:12). Honor each other by listening and not interrupting. Look them in the eye and put your phone away while they are sharing with you. Don't continually pick at what they are doing wrong. You have to let your team make mistakes. Move on and celebrate what they do well. When you ask a volunteer to do a task, and then go and redo it yourself because you like the way you do it better, you are in pride. They won't always get it right like you won't always get it right, so be forgiving and flexible enough to move forward and not get stuck in offense. Living offended will slow down your fruitfulness.

Be patient. Don't get upset if members of your team don't put out as much as you do. Some are fast, some take their time, and some are better at certain things than others, but it's not a competition. You will have volunteers who will do more than the others, which has the potential to create some conflict. Just be watching for the enemy's tactics. "For we wrestle not against flesh and blood, but against principalities, against powers, against the rulers of the darkness of this world, against spiritual wickedness in high places" (Eph. 6:12, *KJV*). The devil will always be trying to get you to be against people and the way they operate. As a leader, you can suggest different ways of doing things and oversee the project, but don't hover in control. Learn to overlook some things and assign different projects to other volunteers if needed. Don't make a big deal out of something that can be easily fixed or changed. Above all, pray for them and thank God that He chose you to lead the group of volunteers that have come to serve.

If correction or direction is needed, be firm, but I encourage you to be kind in your delivery. Volunteers are God's kids, too, and how you treat them is much more important to God than you might think. If you know you have a strong personality, tone it down when you have a problem with someone or with what they are doing. If you're softer, have the courage to say what is needed and don't be intimated by them. "A soft answer turns away wrath, but a harsh word stirs up anger" (Prov. 15:1, *NKJV*). Speak honestly and openly and spend some time in prayer before you approach them to start the conversation, being "quick to listen, slow to speak, and slow to get angry" (Jas. 1:19, *NLT*). Remember, they could be potential future leaders and pastors, so be a good example for them. Lead them into Him. Most likely, the Holy Spirit has already been dealing with them about the issue before you ever got there. Listen to Him on how, or if, He would like you to correct them in each situation. It will go better that way. Treat them well.

A volunteer is to assist your team, but they shouldn't be lazy. Train them in doing things the right way. Lead them in the preparation time, and work together to accomplish what needs to get done. There is nothing worse than a haphazard, slapped-together project, and if things are half done when the kids come, it is not a good reflection on you, your team, or the ministry. Do things well, and with quality, and purpose. After the youth night or event is over, clean up and try not to leave it for another day whenever possible.

You will probably have some volunteers that get along really well with each other. Awesome! It is so nice to have a group working together and serving alongside each other for Jesus. But, sometimes, team members can start congregating in groups off to the side apart from the kids to hang out and chat. It's very easy to do. Who doesn't want to share a joke or story with their peers? Just watch the frequency on how often it is happening. You are all there to serve the teens, and for the few short hours you have per week with them, everyone's focus should be on talking to the kids and hanging out with them. Some of the best conversations and breakthroughs can happen during that hang-out time when you have just a few minutes with a teenager to hear what they are going through or to pray with them. It's worth every second. After the kids have left, you and the other leaders are free to hang out with each other as much as you like.

Do your best to keep the kids' personal information they share with you to yourself and your team if they need to know. When a teenager shares something about their past or current situation, it's an honor to be there to help them turn to Jesus with it all. They will look to you and the other volunteers often as the ones who can fix their problems but God is the One who delivers, saves, and has the answers. If you or your leaders begin talking about the kids in public, or start sharing their story with someone else, it breaks trust.

When that teenager finds out you said something they didn't want you to share, they won't tell you anything anymore. "A talebearer reveals secrets, but he who is of a faithful spirit conceals a matter" (Prov. 11:13, *NKJV*). Be honorable and learn how to have some self-control and not tell everything you hear. Talk to the Lord about it instead and pray for those kids in what they are going through.

Tell your team to save every text conversation they get from a teenager, whether it's just a message or anything over social media. Today, we need to be smart about what is said, and evidence needs to be produced if ever asked for or required. Most of the time this shouldn't be an issue, but the odd case may come up where parents or certain authorities are involved, and the whole truth needs to be shared. Remember, there are always two sides to every story, and yours is only half of it. Your conversations over a screen should be biblical help. Teenagers are minors, and the right boundaries need to be in place and respected. Keep your senior pastor in the loop if you don't know how to deal with a problem or if a parent or guardian gets involved over a conversation you had with their teen. Pay special attention to the Lord's voice in these circumstances.

Commitment. Different people have different ideas of what that word means, but it comes down to simply doing what you said you would do. If a volunteer said they would be there, they should be there—on time and at the place. If they said they would take care of something, they should do it. If they get in a bind beforehand, they need to let you know. Emergencies can only happen so often; no one should be leaving you stranded for help week after week. You will quickly learn who you can rely on and who you can trust. Teach your team what it means to give their word and how Jesus showed us what it looks like. Lead them in what it means to be committed, dedicated, and loyal.

Bringing in new volunteers can ruffle feathers with both your current staff and your teenagers. It will take time for them to trust the new person coming in, so be patient and always highlight the new person's strengths in front of the kids. Give the new team member opportunities to dive right into what you have going on. The more involved they become, the quicker the teens will get to know them and accept the change. Your teenagers need to know there will never be a carbon copy of you, and that there are qualities in this new person that you will never have. Each volunteer needs to be appreciated and accepted for who they are. The kids make up their minds pretty quickly about someone, so prepare your new volunteer as much as you can by communicating to them how the group is used to operating. Reassure the kids that things may shift a little bit, but that it will be for the better.

Your leadership team will more than likely change many times over the years. It can be hard to say goodbye to the youth leaders that have served so faithfully. There can also be others that were more challenging to work alongside, making their exit from the group uncomfortable. There are many transitions that have not been done well in ministry. It's the enemy's plan to divide, and many have left out of offense and bitterness. We can prevent a lot of this from happening in managing how we treat people and in what we say. But you may come across some really difficult conflicts. Even Barnabas and Paul had strife between them, and "the contention became so sharp that they parted from one another" (Acts 15:39, *NKJV*). Remember this—it doesn't matter the reason for the exit, it matters that *you* do the right thing. "If it is possible, as much as depends on you, live peaceably with all men" (Rom. 12:18, *NKJV*). Keep your heart right before God, and make sure your conscience is clear and void of any offense you may have picked up. Clear the air between you and the volunteer leaving if it needs cleared. Be sure to thank them for all their time, energy, and service for the Kingdom and send them off well.

Raise up the Joshua's of this generation—the faithful leaders who come to serve. Moses spent time with Joshua in training and teaching, so he was prepared when Moses' time was up. One of your volunteers may one day replace your position, so lead them well. Train them in the admonition of the Lord. Encourage them in their gifting to minister and let them use what they have on the inside of them. They are never going to be exactly like you, so don't mold them into your shape and form because they will have their own. Celebrate the way that God has made them and help them heed the direction they need to take. If one of your volunteers steps into your position, take your hands off the wheel, and step far enough back so they can grow into what they are called to be. It's time for you to do something different.

Speak well of your team and the people you serve with. The more you magnify what is right and what is going well, the better things will be. Look at how Jesus treated his team of disciples, the way He led, and the things that were done. He is our ultimate example so let us, "Therefore be imitators of God, as beloved children. And walk in love, as Christ loved us and gave himself up for us, a fragrant offering and sacrifice to God" (Eph. 5:1-2, *ESV*). Seasons come and go. Appreciate your volunteers while they are with you, it's only for a time. What a privilege to work with others in the body of Christ to serve this generation of souls!

Chapter 4

The Parents

We live in an age where the average family is running five different directions fitting in as many activities as possible, and youth group usually happens to just be another thing on that list. I had some parents who wanted to be involved with youth and were interested in the events and if help was needed, but I never actually met most parents. They dropped their kid off at the door, headed to their next activity, and were back to pick them up when youth was done. Standing in the parking lot to say hi or waving as they drove off was the extent of the contact I had with most of them. I was just thankful they took the time to bring their teenagers and that they trusted me to teach them.

A benefit of being a youth pastor is that many teenagers will be open to receive from you a little more easily because you aren't their parent or teacher at school telling them what to do. However, this still does not make you the most important adult in their life. Use this open door to help encourage these kids to have good relationships with their parents in the way the Word encourages them to do so. "Children, obey your parents in the Lord, for this is right. "Honor your father and mother," which is the first commandment with promise: that it may be well with you, and you may live long on the earth" (Eph. 6:1-3, *NKJV*). Teach them how to honor their parents, to pray for them, and to not criticize or yell at them. Every few months I would have the kids write down on a recipe card the top three things they were currently struggling with. On average, 70% of them would write down that they were having trouble with their parents. Your kids need to know that their parent is not their enemy and that things can be better if they are willing to cooperate and do things God's way.

Having some form of communication with the parents needs to be implemented, but you will have to be satisfied with the amount of response you receive. Most parents simply don't want another letter, email, or text to read. I started a group message chat on an app that would allow the parents to control how many notifications they would receive, and that seemed to work pretty well. They could read and respond when it was convenient for them rather than feel pressured to reply as soon as possible. At the very least, parents should know how to reach you: office number, email, or cell phone. Reassure parents that you are available and when you are available. It could be before or after youth group or let them know there is always an opportunity to meet somewhere during the week to discuss any concerns they may have.

Some parents will be cautious about what your youth group all entails. Answer their questions to the best of your ability and reassure them that their teenager is in capable hands. The more hesitant parents are usually first timers who have never let their child attend a youth group before. Typically, after the first few weeks, they will have backed off and won't be as concerned anymore. I had one parent who wanted to sit in on a regular Bible Study night and observe which was fine with me. I see no problem with a parent attending once or twice to see what's going on if they want to be informed of what their son or daughter is involved in. However, when there is a parent in the room watching everything, everyone's aware of it. It takes away the free atmosphere and puts somewhat of a damper on the night.

Part of the appeal of even going to a youth group as a teenager is that parents aren't there, and it should remain that way. My recommendation is that unless they are part of your team or volunteering, youth group should have just teenagers attending.

There are great parents out there who will volunteer to help with just about anything. Thank God for them! They are great servants for the Kingdom, and it takes a load off your back with all the extra duties that surround a youth group. I found it especially helpful when parents volunteered to drive the kids around or organize a side event. What a blessing to have help! I had one mom that would randomly bring extra food in now and then and message me links on different kinds of youth games that might be fun. It was so thoughtful and helpful!

When you have events that aren't at the church, it's important to stick to what is scheduled and be back on time. Don't leave parents waiting in the parking lot for their teenager. When you set a time to return to the church, make sure it's earlier and not later. I ran into a few nights where we were a bit later than expected. Sometimes it was because of road conditions in the winter or an unexpected drop-off along the way, but I needed to take those factors into consideration before landing in the parking lot too late. Part of preparing for youth outings is foreseeing any factors that could change your scheduled departure and arrival time. No parent wants to wait longer than the time designated. Being timely is the honorable thing to do. Should a sudden change in schedule happen to you, send a quick text or call the parents to keep them aware.

One thing I wanted to do was hold a Parents' Appreciation Night at the church to say thank you for letting their teenager come to youth, which also would have given the chance to get to know them better. It's another thing to add to the ever-growing "list," but a great idea to incorporate. I found that the more the parents were involved with what their child was doing, the better life was for everyone. There are lots of great ideas out there about how to connect parents with their teenagers. Anything that promotes and builds relationships is a good thing in my book.

When a teenager says, "My Mom and Dad won't care," there may be some validity to their claim, but you should always call and check with the parent regardless of the scenario. I would often drive kids home after youth group, and I made sure their parents knew where I was at and when I was leaving the church with their child. After trust was built there was less need for communication, but there should be a good understanding between you and the parents to begin with. It never hurts to double check and make sure.

As youth pastor, you are not to go behind the parents' backs and do something they expressly don't want done for their child. For example, if you have planned a youth group water baptism day and a parent doesn't want their son or daughter baptized, then you must respect their wishes. The teenager may really want to be baptized, and, of course, you will want it for them as well, but you cannot supersede the wishes of the parent. Always respect what the parent has asked of you. Most parents aren't bothered with what you plan or do, but the odd one will be a lot more attentive to what's going on and will want to be informed on any decisions that you make.

If a teenager attends your church on a regular basis, do your best to say hi to their families on the days you have services. This will help establish a friendly familiarity. Say hi to the younger siblings as well. These kids are excited to be around you, and they will tell you how many years they have left before they get to join youth group, too! Give them high-fives or wave at them from across the room. Future teenagers coming right up!

Attend your kids' sports games, band concerts, or other school events if you can. It's an opportunity to be around their parents and extended family. Sometimes that was all the interaction I had with the parents for the entire school year. That time with them was important to me because their teenager was important to me. Being trusted by them to teach their child about the Lord was such a gift. We would watch and cheer from the sidelines while having great conversation about their kids. Getting to know the parents helps you understand where their teenagers are coming from. Do your best to thank them for bringing their son or daughter to youth group.

You will quickly find that a lot of your teenagers are coming from broken homes. It seems rare these days to find someone who grew up in a family with two parents who loved each other, are still together, and maintain a healthy and happy home. Youth group could quite possibly be the only place they feel safe all week. I've heard countless stories of teens sharing that youth group is what saved them in high school from going off the deep end. You truly won't realize the impact youth group has on some of your kids until much later down the road. When you teach them and love them week after week, the love of Jesus will curl around their heart and heal their brokenness. Your youth group is often a haven and a refuge for those kids without you even knowing it.

A sobering reality is that bad parents do exist. Parents in jail, parents who sexually abuse their children, beat them, alcoholics, drug addicts, the list goes on and on. If a teenager is unsafe at home, let that teenager know they can text or call you if they are having trouble with a parent or think something bad might happen. Make sure the teenagers are safe, but do not try to take care of something on your own. Your senior pastor is someone who needs to know about the situation. Abuse is something that you are mandated to report to authorities in many circumstances, so be aware of the guidelines in your county and state or province. So many kids grow up without a good parent, and if they attend your youth group, they will be desperate for some answers. Point them to the ultimate father figure—God Himself. When the lightbulb comes on that God is not like their mom or dad and that He is always good, it will bring great comfort. This world is not without its devastation and tragedy, but the glory and healing of the Lord Jesus far outshines any circumstance someone has been through.

An incredibly important key to remember is that there are always two sides to every story. Your teenagers will confide in you and share some negative things going on at home, but keep in mind that the parent has the other side of the story, and will probably have quite a different perspective. You won't get to hear the parents' side most of the time unless they come in for counsel or pull you aside after a youth night. Know that teenagers in general won't always tell the truth and they can exaggerate things, so listen for the Lord's direction in how He wants you to handle these situations. Parents aren't exempt from lying, but you are not to pick sides; you are to help all of them and give biblical counsel.

When a teenager trusts you and tells you what's going on at home, your protective streak might come out. You will have moments of being really upset with how the parent has been acting, but this is obviously none of your business. Watch that you don't take sides with the teenager against the parents and have hard feelings against them yourself. Remain in the love walk and forgive the parent for what they have done to their child or the things they have said. I had quite a few teenagers who were heartbroken over the fact that their parents said they were a mistake, that they would never get anywhere in life, or that they were just like their mom or dad. Parents make mistakes. God has forgiven us of much, so we ought to forgive each other, too. Remember to "be kind to one another, tenderhearted, forgiving one another, as God in Christ forgave you" (Eph. 4:32, *ESV*).

Some of the parents will be quite broken themselves. They may, or may not, know Jesus and be barely holding it together. Just because they are dropping their kid off in the parking lot at church doesn't mean they know God themselves or that they are driving away perfectly happy and content. There is often a major crisis you won't know about. Even though your primary ministry is to their daughter or son, there is a chance you may get to minister to the mom or dad as well. Sometimes they just need prayer and someone to understand what they are going through. I would have nights where the kids would be the ones waiting in the car, while I was talking and praying with their parents in the kitchen. You aren't limited to just teenagers; you are allowed to help parents, too. Encourage them and pray for them along with their teenager.

Most of your teenagers will be future parents. Chances are that some of them have made inner vows that they will never be like one of their parents because of how they were treated or disciplined. This can be a dangerous trap to fall into. We simply cannot be perfect or never make a mistake again. Your kids need to know that while they may succeed in ways their parents did not, they will make other mistakes in areas where their parents never did. Inner vows are never the answer, relationship with God is. He will show you how to be the best parent you can be and give you the grace and mercy you need when you don't deserve it.

Some of your teenagers may already be parents. It is not an abnormal thing to have a pregnant teen in a youth group. I never had one of my teenagers bring their baby to Bible Study, so this is a bridge you will have to cross if you come to it, but the one who is pregnant needs to know that she is loved by God regardless of her pregnancy or previous decisions she has made. I often told my kids if anyone got pregnant and was thinking of aborting to please go through with the pregnancy because I would keep and raise their baby or help them find someone who would. They were usually quite surprised at this statement, but I meant it with all my heart. Abortion is the death of a child created by God who deserves to live a life on this earth. Satan has stolen and lied and killed many, many babies on this planet for thousands of years. We need to protect the unborn as much as we possibly can. Speak life into those young parents. They will be forced to grow up quickly.

I was single the entire time I was a youth pastor, and there were pros and cons when it came to having no parental experience. Because I wasn't married with kids, I was single like the rest of my teenagers and our common ground helped me relate with them on many levels. We understood each other. I was familiar with the pressure that came from peers, the desire to want to be with someone, and I knew what it was like to feel alone. I wasn't their parent, so I never took that role on unknowingly because I simply didn't know how to be that for them in the first place. However, being single meant I missed some important things such as checking with the parents first before asking the teenager to volunteer or come early to help with something. Having team leaders and volunteers that were already parents helped me close the gap in many areas where I lacked experience. I picked up some basic principles from them in what parents need to know and was thankful for the help in the places where I was weak.

Parents are just as important as teenagers, especially in God's eyes. While you navigate relationships with both parties, always refer back to the ultimate parent/child relationship—the one we have with our Father God. He is our example of what a good parent looks like, and He's got so much grace to extend to His kids. Thank God often that the parents of your teenagers bring them to youth group and trust you to teach their kids. It is a privilege to have a part in training up this next generation for the Lord. Let's do it well.

Chapter 5

The Games & Snacks

Youth group needs to be fun! If it's not fun, teenagers probably won't come. They are required to go to school, but they don't have to come to youth group. If they come, it's because they want to be there. There will be kids that *have* to come to youth because their parents make them, but this is beside the point. You can't have everything be serious and overly disciplined. It just won't fly. You won't have kids the next week, and you will realize you might need to adjust some things. Youth group needs a lot of laughter, a lot of smiles, and a lot of fun. Games and snacks are part of that equation.

Filling the kids' stomachs with pizza and Dr. Pepper became quite the staple for our group. Your church's budget will determine a lot of what you can and cannot do. Feeding the kids week after week gets expensive, and you need to be on the same page with your senior pastor on what you are allowed to spend in that area. I would often pre-order earlier in the day and get one of the volunteers to pick up the pizza on their way to the church. If money is not an issue, pre-ordering pizza is the quickest and easiest way to feed the teenagers on youth night. Half the time I would bake some in our church's oven while all the kids showed up. Our youth group always hung out in the kitchen area of our church, so while the pizzas baked, it was the perfect opportunity to go around and chat with everyone while we all waited for a slice of pepperoni.

If money is tight, you might be able to get some of the kids, their parents, or even congregation members involved in a rotating schedule for bringing snacks. There was one lady in our church that offered to bake brownies for my teenagers every week for several years. It was such a blessing, and the kids loved them. Another wanted to cook supper for the group, so we incorporated that into Bible Study night. She loved serving in this way, and she was a great fit with the kids as well. Food can be an awesome opportunity to incorporate other giftings in the body, and being able to fellowship around a table while enjoying a meal is a blessing.

You usually become a youth pastor with a picture in your mind of standing in front of kids with your Bible and teaching them about Jesus—not necessarily getting plastered with water balloons thrown at you from across the parking lot. Welcome to youth ministry! Most of the time leading up to your teaching will be filled with opportunities to plant seeds in those kids, and playing games just happens to be one of them. You might as well get used to the fact that you will be doing a lot of running around, throwing things, hiding in places that are hard to get out of, and perhaps even having the odd whipped cream pie shoved in your face. Be ready for it all and get right in there with them! They will love you for it.

Surprisingly, I found the prep for the games to be a very time-consuming part of youth ministry, but one of the most necessary components. We were constantly trying to find which games would or would not work with our group. Thankfully, there are an abundance of resources out there that make this job easier, but it still takes time to find them. Certain groups of kids will like certain games, and then the next group will not like them at all. Don't get discouraged when what you find does not end up working. There is no formula. You can't ever nail down a good enough plan where the same thing will work year after year no matter what. That's just not youth ministry. When things totally flop, laugh about it! So what if it didn't work out like you thought? Try again with a fresh idea, or better yet, have the kids come up with something new! They are full of ideas, and when you get them involved in planning things for their group, some leadership skills will float to the surface and their confidence in what God has gifted them in will be brought out into the light.

There will always be kids that don't want to join in at game time. It's inevitable. Whether they are uncertain and don't like to try new things, or say they aren't feeling well, you need to discern what's going on and do your best to get them to participate. The negative aspect of a kid refusing to join the game is that they draw attention toward them while everyone is waiting to start. When the other teens see them not participating, some will want to waver from the group and join them on the sidelines. To be honest, what I often did was give them no choice in the matter. I would kindly walk over to them and say, "You're coming! You're my partner!" They will have plenty of excuses and reasons why they don't want to join, but most of it just comes out of insecurity and not knowing what to expect. Of course, there is the aspect of if they are physically not able to play, but in general, everyone should be able to participate.

The building space you have will often determine what types of games you are able to play. Our youth group met in our church's kitchen and dining room area. It was great for snacks, pizza, and hang out time, but not so great for games. We did as many outdoor activities as we possibly could until the weather changed and the snow fell, then it was back to indoors and circle games with a lot of sitting. Teenagers can be hard on a building. Things seem to get broken regardless of trying to be careful, so just do the best you can and leave the rough play for outdoors. If you've got a designated youth room, or even a gym, that's awesome! Make the best use of the space that you have.

Every teenager seems to have a cell phone these days. Use them. Instead of constantly telling them to put their phones down and join in, use them in game time. Create a scavenger hunt around your church building with pictures of random items they must find and take pictures to prove they found them. Use the phones for funny two-minute plays where they act out Bible stories, and later have a watch party to judge which one is the winner. Have them text you the best pictures of the night so you can post them on your youth group's Instagram story. Get creative and use what everyone already has in their hands. They get told all day long to put their phones away. Who knows? Some of your kids might have future jobs in social media and youth group videos are one step in how they get there. God has some interesting things up His sleeve.

Make use of the holidays. When Christmas came, we played Christmas games. We wrapped up people in wrapping paper and had a contest for the best looking "gift." When Valentine's Day came, we would play "Honey, if You Love Me," and laugh hysterically at faces turning beet red as the kids did their best to maintain their serious expression while getting called "honey" by peers kneeling in front of them. Get some variety in there! Don't just do the same old same old (unless it's working for you and the kids love it), but make the effort to find new ideas. If there's snow outside, get everyone to bring their winter gear, slide down some hills, or have a contest with the best-looking snowman. If it's hot out, get the water balloons ready and be prepared to get wet. These types of days make the greatest memories.

Get right in there and join your kids in playing games. This is important. It is way more fun when the youth pastor joins in, and you truly do make it more exciting for them. You will lose their enthusiasm by telling them to go outside and play while you get things ready indoors. Have things ready as much as possible beforehand so both you and your other leaders can be with the kids the entire time you have them. Walk with them, talk with them, laugh with them, play games with them. If there are a couple different games going on between multiple groups, spend a bit of time playing in each of them, or cheer for them on the sidelines. Get involved as much as you can!

Have a collection of sports equipment for your group that includes basketballs, volleyballs, tennis balls, footballs, and frisbees. You will probably use them all. It's also handy to have an air pump for when balls go flat. Purchasing some small orange cones to use as boundary lines was a must have, especially when we brought them to joint events with the other youth groups in town. We used different colored bandanas for distinguishing between teams and tied them around our belt loops. Lots of creative ideas can be used. Make sure the kids help you clean up at the end and get everything back in its place.

The amount of physical contact between teenagers is something to keep an eye on. Games usually involve touch of some sort—you can't get away from that component. But try to make sure everyone is acting as decently as possible. Today, something can blow up at a moment's notice with some teen telling their parent that you or someone else touched them inappropriately. This is where the Holy Spirit will be warning you ahead of time, helping you with what actions you may need to take. Most of the time this won't be an issue—they already have gym class at school and know not to be touching other people inappropriately. I recommend no-tackle football just in case, though!

Sometimes, a movie night is a refreshing change of pace. Be sure to watch the movie yourself before showing it to the kids. It was always interesting to note that when we announced a movie night, we would get kids coming that never came to any of our other youth events. So, pop the popcorn and hand out the Dr. Pepper! Praise the Lord that even a movie is something to draw kids to Jesus. There are some powerful movies coming out so take advantage of that. You may have to keep an eye on how many are going to the bathroom during the show. Looking back now, I probably should have had an intermission of sorts so they weren't getting into trouble for being gone too long and getting into something they shouldn't be. Watch how dark the room is as well. It is nice to have the lights out when a movie is playing, but when it comes to a bunch of teenage guys and girls in the same room, you need to play it smart.

When you get into the senior youth age of teens, the games tend to get less popular. I found that the older ones are more interested in talking with their friends and hanging out than kicking a ball around every single week. The junior youth ages need the games to run off steam, but the senior youth are usually just fine with a more laid-back evening. The indoor game of "Four on a Couch" was forever a hit with my older teens. We had a lot of laughter and looks from across the room with circle games. Depending on the ages of your group, and how many guys there are versus girls, prepare to be flexible. Just roll with who you have and adjust as necessary.

Sometimes we had kids that just wanted to come for the food and games, and then purposely leave before the Bible Study portion began. Again, they will have excuses why they are leaving, and you need to be wise in these instances. If they said a parent wants them home, get ahold of the parent on the phone right then. They need to know that if they are coming to youth group they need to stay for the whole thing and not just the parts they like. If you don't check into what they are doing, you will have a teen off doing who knows what, and you and their parent not knowing where they are at. Do a head count if needed because you are the one responsible for these kids for the few hours you have them. Be in charge and be wise. Usually it will be a sports practice, band concert, or some school event where a teenager needs to leave early. If that's the case, ask them to inform you as soon as they arrive at youth. You can clear it with their parents if necessary, and they can have fun until it's time for them to go.

In all my years of youth pastoring, we only had one major accident during game time that I can remember. A volunteer had to take one of the kids to the ER for a cut on their hand. Thankfully, the parents were glad everything was handled so well, and the teenager had a new story to tell everyone. It's wise to have a first aid kit somewhere on the property along with a plan of action in case something happens, but also realize that this is where prayer and laying hands on the sick immediately comes in. The Bible tells us that "these signs shall follow them that believe...they shall lay hands on the sick, and they shall recover" (Mark 16:17-18, *KJV*). We have so many promises from God on His protection and His angels that keep watch over us, like in Psalm 91:11-12: "For he shall give his angels charge over you, to keep you in all your ways. In their hands they shall bear you up, lest you dash your foot against a stone" (*NKJV*). Run straight over to the person who is hurt and immediately lay your hands on the teenager in the Name of Jesus. So much can be taken care of in the spirit while the natural is being ministered to at the same time. I know our protection throughout the years was not only our team doing their part to keep everyone safe, but the amount of prayer that went forth on behalf of those kids. God kept us protected on every side.

Overall, you will have a blast with your kids playing games. Keep it fun and lighthearted and be willing to laugh at yourself and look ridiculous in front of everyone. Be an example to the teenagers of good sportsmanship. Not everyone has to be athletic to have a good time playing a game. I was probably the least athletic one out there, but making the effort to get right in with them and having them teach me a thing or two was a lot of fun! Remember, it's a tool that can be used to get hearts ready to hear the Gospel, so work with the Lord on this. It may be your least favorite thing you do in your role as youth pastor, but do it for Jesus. "...whatever you do, do it heartily, as to the Lord and not to men" (Col. 3:23 *NKJV*).

Chapter 6

The Studying & Teaching

Some of the greatest wisdom I ever received was to always ask the Lord what He wants you to teach. If you minister on what *you* think teenagers need to hear, you will miss the mark. Are there plenty of things we think they should know and be doing? Absolutely. Does the Holy Spirit know better in this area? Yes. He knows exactly where their hearts are at, what they are personally struggling with, and what they need in the moment. If we, as leaders, plow in there and teach them what *we* think they need to know, that's pride, and the outcome won't be what you expect. We need to watch that we aren't assuming things and judging based on what we see happening in their lives in the natural. Lay down your ideas, your thoughts, and your attitudes to be a vessel for God to move through.

Everyone has a different way of studying and teaching. You might do really well in putting together a teaching series that will last several weeks, or you may enjoy studying a variety of topics. Find comfortability in what way you study and flow in that. There would usually be a topic that God would have me focus on such as relationships, hearing God, purpose in life, parents, etc. I would often look up definitions, think of personal examples, and find a Bible story that would fit well. Occasionally, I would hear absolutely nothing from God on what to teach, so I would either pick something, or just spend time praying in the Spirit over what was going to happen that night. Often, just sitting and being quiet before the Lord led me to some of the greatest lessons I ever taught. "I will bless the Lord who has given me counsel; my heart also instructs me in the night seasons" (Psa. 16:7, *NKJV*).

Make sure you leave plenty of time for preparing your message and watch that you don't procrastinate and throw something together at the last minute. To minister effectively and walk in the power of the Holy Spirit requires faithfulness, diligence, and preparation. It always amazed me how many calls, texts, and "pressing" needs came up the day services were scheduled. We have an enemy that doesn't like us to be in the Word, and he will bring distraction from unexpected places. You know yourself and your habits, so just be smart and do your best to overcome areas in your life that may be weak. It will only happen with the Holy Spirit's help. Keep your phone on silent, find a place where you can be alone, and do what you can in the natural to protect your time with the Lord.

The message portion of the night is incredibly important and should last longer than ten minutes. Too many youth groups have their attention and focus on the games and pizza, leaving the Bible time until the very end, if at all. This should not be. Your kids need foundation in the Word and biblical instruction so that they can know how to live their lives as Christ followers. They need to understand their identity in Him and form their own relationship with their heavenly Father. Hearing the Word preached (Rom. 10:17) brings the faith that is needed to walk out their purpose in this life (Gal. 2:20). Youth group is a fun place to be, but it's got to incorporate the needed teaching for spiritual growth to occur. We all need this daily bread from heaven (Matt. 6:11). Pour the scriptures into them so they can live their lives for the Lord Jesus Christ. Disciple and teach them well.

The way you teach will differ from other leaders, and that is completely normal. God made you who you are on purpose and gifted you a certain way. If you try to copy someone else's style, it's like walking in a pair of shoes that are too big. Walk in your own gifting and thank God for it. I personally liked having a bit of interaction between the kids and I during the message, and I enjoyed when they had questions or when other topics would come up so we could run a rabbit trail or two. If you like using a whiteboard or enjoy having a PowerPoint to keep you on track, that's good, too. A lot of people are visual learners, so it's always nice to have some key points to look at. Sometimes an object lesson can be one of the best tools or even acting out a Bible story can be fun. Whatever way you present the Gospel, do it well, and do it all for the glory of God.

There will be nights where you need to be ready to completely change what you're going to speak on. Some days I would study a certain topic and get all excited about sharing it only to have God change the entire message the second I opened my mouth to speak. He knows what those kids need to hear, and He needs you flexible enough to adapt to His direction. It actually gets kind of fun! Ministering by faith under the anointing and following the Holy Ghost's direction for your youth group is much more important than what you may have planned. In fact, some days my entire study time was God working on me in a specific area of my personal life while I was thinking it would be for my teenagers. Youth group time would come, and none of what I had studied would even make it into the message that night, but I knew God was adjusting some things in me that needed to be brought to light. The time you take to study is so valuable. The Holy Ghost knows what is best for you and for the teens.

One night, the topic for our Bible Study went in the direction of abortion. I tried to direct it back to what I had studied about that day, but God kept bringing me to the subject of abortion instead. Many of the kids began to ask questions from all different angles, and then a new girl in the back put up her hand. She asked if aborted babies went to heaven. I told her they absolutely do and shared about the age of accountability and the mercy of God. The visible relief on her face, and the quiet witness on the inside of me, showed me why God was wanting it discussed. This girl was on the verge of tears the whole night, but when the grace and forgiveness of God was shared, the freedom came, and I could sense her burden had been lifted by the Blood. Thank God for His Word and the freedom it will bring. May we all yield to Him more and more.

As a youth pastor, you will find that you can't just walk into a room full of teenagers, start teaching, and expect them to receive well from you. There's more to it than just that. You have to *know* them. What was their day like? What are they going through? Is there something bothering them that they need help with? You may have the best message and be the greatest teacher, but if you don't personally care about them as individuals, that great message will fall on deaf ears. You have to genuinely care, and when they know that you do, they will receive what you have to say so much better. Be moved with compassion as Jesus was (Matt. 9:36).

I found that my teenagers could usually handle about 30-40 minutes of speaking on average. Don't make it about length and think that the more you speak, the more they are going to get. Often, a shorter message that is packed with the meat of the Word will bear more fruit than something you go on and on about just trying to fill up time. Attention span is probably the shortest it's ever been in history. Scrolling for hours on social media and taking in massive amounts of information in very short increments is the world we live in now. Regardless, God still reaches people and can download something into them in a moment that might have taken a year of teaching to understand. He is not bound by our time. Having the right word at the right moment is our aim.

Every couple of months I would have a question-and-answer night, and it seemed to work extremely well. The kids would write down the top three things they were struggling with on a recipe card (no name necessary), and then I would teach them off of what they wrote on the cards. Great topics and discussions came out of those nights and they received answers to questions they would never want to ask out loud. Some of your biggest, toughest teenagers who you don't think will admit to struggling with anything will write down some pretty serious things. Be prayed up and prepared to minister out of the overflow. Ask God for His answers and watch that your opinions don't try to take the spotlight. "I don't know" is a perfectly acceptable response. You don't know everything and it's okay not to.

Splitting up the guys and girls every few months worked well. There are just some topics that don't need to be discussed in front of both genders. Girls need to be encouraged to wait for the right guy and that her identity is not in the clothes she wears, the hairstyles she picks, or in giving herself away. Guys need to know what it looks like to respect the girls, what it means to be a Godly leader, and that they are enough. Sometimes having the female leaders teach the guys and the male leaders teach the girls can also be beneficial. Let them ask whatever they want. Be open enough to share about some things in your past and how God brought you through. You obviously aren't required to do so, but sharing personal stories always makes a significant impact.

I would usually teach at least once a year on dating and saving yourself for marriage. You are teaching the prime age group where hormones are raging and physical boundary lines are being crossed. The statistics of high school students who graduate having already been sexually active are sobering. Celebrate virginity, purity, and saving yourself for marriage. Teach them on God's covenant design. Your teenagers need to know that others are in the same boat, and that they aren't the only ones who haven't had sex. At the same time, reassure the ones who have already been sexually active of God's mercy and forgiveness and that what they did is covered by the Blood. There is a lot of grace and mercy from our Father, and they don't need to live in shame. Pick them back up with words of life from the Bible and encourage them to live pure before God.

Many, many topics will be taught and discussed week after week, and you need to keep in mind to never judge how it's going by the looks on the kids' faces. If you do, you will be easily discouraged. Some will look like they absolutely disagree with what you are saying, but will come up to you later and comment on how great it was. Others will look like they are getting it and miss most everything you said. Certain kids will have their heads down looking at their phones so you may need to have a bucket to drop cell phones in so they will actually pay attention. Others can handle not looking at their screens during the lesson. It all just depends on the group you have. They will make comments on not liking a topic that you teach, or have remarks on how you already taught that. Don't worry about it. "Preach the Word! Be ready in season and out of season" (2 Tim. 4:2, *KJV*). Do what the Holy Spirit asks of you—nothing more, nothing less.

Talk about the real issues that teenagers deal with on a regular basis. Sex, drugs, porn, addiction, homosexuality, masturbation, alcohol, suicide, teen pregnancy, kids that want to be transgender, the list goes on. You need to be okay with addressing the hard topics from a biblical perspective. I remember asking my kids how often they got teased about being a virgin at school, and they said it happens every day. Every. Day. We cannot shy away from any topic, especially in the days we are living right now. Teenagers need to hear the truth and they need to hear it sooner rather than later. If you think they don't know about something yet, think again. All they have to do is open their phone and in five seconds have any type of information they want. Fill them up with "the Way, the Truth, and the Life" (John 14:6, *KJV*).

As my pastor often told me, be pleasantly surprised when people do the right thing. Without realizing it, we often set high expectations of what we think others should be doing. When those expectations go unfulfilled, disappointment comes and we feel let down. Leave your pride at the door. Our job is not to put pressure on teenagers (or anybody) to make them change. Our job is to put pressure on our covenant with God and intercede for them in prayer because "the effectual fervent prayer of a righteous man availeth much" (Jas. 5:16, *KJV*). Your teenagers will make mistakes. No one on this earth is perfect. You will find yourself teaching them one thing and the next week getting a text or call from them in tears saying they did the exact opposite of what was taught. They will be struggling with the guilt and shame in their heart so remind them that repentance is a gift. Always restore them back with the words of Jesus and by the reminder "that neither death nor life, nor angels nor principalities nor powers, nor things present nor things to come, nor height nor depth, nor any other created thing, shall be able to separate us from the love of God which is in Christ Jesus our Lord" (Rom. 8:38-39, *NKJV*).

A lot of kids will make great choices. They will hear the Word preached, put it into practice, and bear fruit. Praise the Lord! There is nothing better than one of them sharing with you that they made a step of faith, and how God came through for them! It can be a very simple moment, too, like hearing

God for the first time, praying for a peer, or being able to answer a Bible question someone asked. They all get to hear the Word, and they all get to decide if they will walk it out or not. You can't do it for them, but it's awesome to watch them grow in the Lord and trust God on their own!

One last important key to remember is that whatever you are teaching you should be practicing as well. You can't tell your kids to be doing things that you aren't really walking in yourself, "...for we who teach will be judged more strictly" (Jas. 3:1, *NLT*). This is not to intimidate you or cause you to draw back, but to encourage you to place great value upon the position that God has called you to. You are sowing life changing truths into teenagers and through the help of the Holy Spirit, you will be able to walk out those truths in your own life as well. It is an absolute honor to be an example for young people and to impart into them things that we have learned and walked out in this earth with Jesus. Let's do our best to match our actions with the words that we teach.

Chapter 7

The Counseling

If you ask the majority of teenagers where they get their advice and wisdom, the top three answers will be social media, what they watch online or on tv, and what their friends have to say. They are soaking up hours and hours of entertainment and information, which may or may not be feeding them what their spirits need. Who is the One who can give them direction, bind up their wounds, and heal their broken hearts? His name is Jesus. As a youth pastor, your directive from heaven is to lead these teenagers into relationship with Him. When God becomes their home, their place of influence, their go-to in rough times, they are building their house on The Rock. When the storms of life come, the foundation will be there to withstand the torrents (Matt. 7:24-25). You are a vessel for channeling the wisdom of God into their spirits.

Teaching is one thing, but counseling is another. What you pour out during your teaching time will most likely answer many questions on the inside of the kids, but it doesn't mean that they all listened or heard every word you said. Your kids will come to you and want personal help on their current issues regardless if the answer came out in what you spoke on during Bible Study. They will need prayer, a listening ear, or even a hug. They are sheep that need a shepherd. Value both counseling time in addition to teaching time. Be patient with them as you answer their personal questions and hear what they have to say. After Jesus spoke to the multitudes (Mark 4:34), He would take time with his disciples to answer their questions and dive a bit deeper with them on what He shared publicly. We get to follow His example and do the same with our teenagers.

Your most important job in counseling these kids is to first know the Word for yourself. You want to be able to share accurately what God is wanting you to say. Your experience will speak on many levels, but ultimately, it's the Lord Jesus that is wanting His way in their lives so He can bring them into freedom. Your opinion doesn't matter. You may or may not know what they need, but He does. Every time a teenager asks you a question, don't go back in your brain trying to retrieve a file of what you did when you were that age or what you think they need to hear. You check in with God while they are asking their questions and rely on Him to bring you the words He wants you to say. You are a mediator of sorts, a go-between for the kids and the Father while their steps become more firm in the Lord's way.

Your kids will need counsel in many different areas. They will need to know how to have good relationships, how to successfully navigate their high school season, and to understand what their purpose is, but it goes beyond that. When you have them apart from the group, you will be able to minister to them on a more personal level and share things you wouldn't normally say on a regular Bible Study night. They might be questioning their sexuality, have a porn addiction, or need to give you the razor they have used to cut themselves. This type of vulnerability will come up in private conversation, and counsel is desperately needed in these areas. They need truthful answers apart from what they have already heard the world telling them. Look them in the eye, and be real while you speak the truth in love (Eph. 4:15).

Your heart will hurt for the things your teenagers go through. You will feel somewhat helpless at times because you aren't able to just adopt them and take them all home with you. This is where casting all your care upon Him (1 Ptr. 5:7) comes in. You cannot carry their burden on your shoulders no matter how much you want to. We are not built to be their everything. God needs you to hear what they share, give the counsel that He instructs, and show them the tools necessary to navigate those tough places in their lives. "Come unto Me, all ye that labor and are heavy laden, and I will give you rest. Take my yoke upon you and learn of Me, for I am gentle and lowly in heart, and you will find rest for your souls. For My yoke is easy, and My burden is light" (Matt. 11:28-30, KJV). Let them go to Jesus. Keep that emotional realm in check. Your soul should not be in the lead, it should be following your spirit man. Love them, cry with them, and laugh with them, but let Jesus take their yokes of bondage.

If you don't know the answer to a question they ask you, just be honest and okay with saying that you simply don't know. You can say that you know the One who does. It's actually encouraging when you hear a leader admitting to not knowing it all; it makes them more relatable and less intimidating. Ask the teen to give you some time while you go to God about their question and watch that you actually do that. Follow through, pray into it, and do some homework to study up on what they are wondering about. "Study to show thyself approved unto God, a workman that needeth not to be ashamed, rightly dividing the word of truth" (2 Tim. 2:15, KJV). Talk with your senior pastor as well. The next time you see that teen, you will be able to dive a bit deeper into what their question was, and you will also have learned some things yourself. Win-win.

Every story or problem is worth listening to—once. Some teenagers will only come talk to you because they want attention but this just comes with the territory. Many kids will tell you every single detail of what they are going through while others will only share certain parts. When a teen begins to complain about their problem multiple times this in itself becomes a problem. "Death and life are in the power of the tongue" (Prov. 18:21, *KJV*). Rehearsing a negative issue hinders growth, and you need to lovingly remind them to keep their eyes forward and on Jesus. Mark 11:24 reminds us that God wants us to "speak to the mountain"—speak *to* the problem not *about* it. Disciple them and direct them into learning how to thank God that He is taking care of the issue at hand. Continue pointing them to Jesus so they can know the truth, and the truth will make them free (John 8:32).

God knows exactly how much you should, and should not, share, so if He gives you a check in your spirit mid-sentence, reroute what you were going to say and flow with the river of His Spirit. You may think you have the best Bible counsel for that moment or the greatest example to share, but wait on the Lord so it won't fall on deaf ears. They may not be ready to hear what you have to say or be able to take the Bible knowledge given. Many times, their spirits aren't grown up enough for the real meat, and they just need plain milk. That is 100% okay. Don't force feed them mouthfuls of steak. "As newborn babes, desire the sincere milk of the word, that you may grow thereby" (1 Ptr. 2:2, *KJV*). Give them the milk of the Word at a rate they can manage.

Teenagers are constantly in transition mode. When they come out of their childhood stage into adolescence, it can be challenging to gauge how much information each of them can handle as you counsel. A lot of teens will be more advanced than others. Some will have seen more, heard more, and done more. Others will be on the opposite end of the spectrum and have been brought up in a more sheltered home. Usually, it's the older ones who can handle a lot more, but just say as best as you can what words need to be said to which teenager. Many things you share will be new information to them, and they will in turn share things that will be brand new information to you! You will be continually learning from each other.

Pray at the end of each one-on-one conversation you have with a teenager. Come against the enemy with the Blood and the Name of Jesus. Bind the dark spirits that have hindered them and speak the Word of life into their situation, lay hands on them (Mark 16:18), and believe with them for answers from God. Miracles and breakthrough occur every time you put the Word of God to work and as you pray, it continually guides them back to their Father. Show them how to lay their problems at His feet before the throne. "Let us therefore come boldly to the throne of grace, that we may obtain mercy, and find grace to help in time of need" (Heb. 4:16, *KJV*). When you seal with prayer what you have counseled them on, remind them to pray and talk with God later when they get home. The more familiar they become with prayer, the more comfortable they will be praying on their own.

After you counsel and pray for one of your kids, it may seem like things get worse in their life. Take this as a good sign. Yes, you heard right. When you speak the Word over someone else's life and pray heaven's will into the earth, the devil does not appreciate his ground being taken. Satan will immediately begin to ramp up his game in that person's life with evil tactics, and his forces of darkness will bring temptation and make the situation look like it's worse. His goal is to get the Christian to stop praying. Sadly, many fall for that deception and back off their praying when these obstacles come up thinking that it's not working. They give up what they have set their faith on. DO NOT give in to the enemy's schemes. Put the pressure on your covenant with God and praise in the answers! "And let us not be weary in well doing, for in due season we shall reap, if we faint not" (Gal. 6:9, *KJV*). Don't ever back off no matter what it looks like to you or how much time has gone by.

It's always amazing to me that the most challenging kids come through in the greatest of ways. They will be at the back of the room looking like they don't care about anything you say. It will seem like any counsel you give is going in one ear and out the other. You know that with God there are no hopeless cases, but you sometimes wonder if this particular teenager could fit the bill. Then comes the surprise, a moment with that teen where they tell you they remember everything you say and share that they do, in fact, believe. When they thank you for helping them, it leaves you in wonder at what God did in their heart. They may be rough and frustrating to deal with in front of the other kids for a while, but the Lord has a way of turning them into some of the greatest men and women of God you will ever meet. Stick with them through it all. "Therefore, my beloved brethren, be steadfast, immovable, always abounding in the work of the Lord, knowing that your labor is not in vain in the Lord" (1 Cor. 15:58, *NKJV*).

Don't be checking up on your teenagers to see if they did what you counseled them to do because that's not your job. Let the Holy Spirit work in them and let them make their own choices. If they come back to you needing more help, there might be opportunity to ask if they followed through on the last thing that was said. Other than that, let them go. It's the Holy Spirit's job to convict (John 16:8). No one likes somebody hovering over them, watching their every move. Your teens have a free will just like you do, and they will pick and choose what they want to do without you ever having a say in the matter.

You probably won't have the time to minister one-on-one with every single teen that's in your group, but not every teen needs that one-on-one counsel. A lot of kids will be doing just fine and will receive what they need from the Lord during teaching time. Most of the counsel I gave was first initiated by one of my teenagers either by text or in person. However, I kept an eye on some of the other kids that looked like they were going through a rough time. Many of them are good at hiding it, but the Holy Spirit will point out the one that needs a touch from Him. Follow His prompting and remain approachable.

Be willing to be "on call" when it comes to your kids wanting to communicate with you outside of youth group. Ministry and counseling opportunities are not limited to the few hours you meet up on a Wednesday night. You have the privilege of being someone they might go to if they have a question, or when they get in trouble. There could be a situation that cannot wait a whole week until the next youth night. There is a boundary line here. You do have your own personal life and they don't need to be calling all hours of the day and night, but you want them to be comfortable reaching out to you. This generation is way more comfortable talking over a screen, so use this as an avenue for God. Usually if my teenagers were reaching out to me, they were serious about needing help. I received a number of late-night calls and texts throughout the years and reassured each one that they weren't bothering me. I would tell them to please call me if they were in trouble of any kind, no questions asked. Take the time to reply back if you are able to at the time they text. Remember to offer biblical counsel and be honest with them. Call them if it looks like it could be a lengthy text conversation.

After you counsel one of your teenagers, share the important points with your team if it's something they need to know. You don't need to take the time to go through every detail of what was said, but the important things need to be discussed, especially if the teen is in trouble. When your leaders know what's going on, they will be prepared if that teenager comes to them as well. It's a good thing to share the load and have everybody working together. It makes for a well-functioning group.

The guys usually receive better from a male leader and the girls from a female leader. You are able to counsel the opposite sex, but often there's a lot more understanding between the same gender. This is not a rule to follow, it's just something that seems to work well. When you do counsel the opposite sex, it's a good idea to do it in an area where you can both be physically seen. Pull them aside in the room where everyone else is but far enough away from ears that don't need to hear. It's also wisdom to have another leader join you in that time of counsel if needed. Other leaders in the room will be witnesses in case false accusations are made in how you handled a situation. It would be nice if this wasn't even a concern, but in this day and age, things can get out of hand quickly, and lawsuits aren't fun. Don't be afraid of this, but just be wise.

The Holy Spirit is the ultimate Counselor. He is our example. Remember, He doesn't always say what we want to hear. He's got some tough love with discipline in the mix, but it will bring the results that are needed. "No discipline is enjoyable while it is happening—it's painful! But afterward there will be a peaceful harvest of right living for those who are trained in this way" (Heb. 12:11, *NLT*). Your teenagers will not want to hear some of the things that God wants you to say to them, but you will need to say them anyway. There are some hard things that happen in life that need real and truthful answers. The truth can be difficult to hear, but when it's done in love and in Jesus, growth is the result.

God wants everyone free—free of addiction, bondage, sickness, mental illness, suicidal thoughts, everything that has a stronghold. He "desires all men to be saved and to come to the knowledge of the truth" (1 Tim. 2:4, *NKJV*). When your kids come to you with something on their mind, it is important to the Father so it should also be important to you. There are no dumb questions or invalid issues. Jesus said, "Let the little children come to Me, and do not forbid them; for of such is the kingdom of heaven" (Matt. 19:14, *NKJV*). Value the time you have with each teenager. As youth pastors, we are there to help them.

As you give counsel week after week for the questions, confusion, and hurt, "do it heartily, as to the Lord and not to men" (Col. 3:23, *NKJV*). You are working for God. You are a channel for His love to flow through. Use the Bible to show the teenagers who they really are and how God will bring them through. Encourage, exhort, and lift up the downtrodden. It isn't an accident that you are having a conversation with them or that God has you there to help them. Every one of them is a precious gift from God. Show the teenagers His grace and overflow them with His mercy, for His mercies are new every morning (Lam. 3:22-23).

Chapter 8

LGBTQ

I can remember the day that the kids in my youth group brought up the topic of homosexuality in a manner more serious than before. "Nancy, it's considered cool to be gay at school. What are we supposed to do?" That night there were no teenagers present who identified as LGBTQ. I asked them what percentage of their high school classified themselves as gay or bisexual, and without having to think about it, they replied that it was at least over 50%. I was shocked. I had been out of high school not even a decade at that point and could remember maybe three or four kids out of my entire high school being gay. For the numbers to increase that substantially in just a few years had me taking a way more serious look into it with the Lord than ever before.

Most of the church world has not handled the topic of homosexuality very well. They have either avoided it altogether not knowing what to say, or they have shamed anyone who has even mentioned the thought of struggling with same sex attraction. Things that have been hidden for centuries are now in the spotlight and openly praised on many platforms, but the truth is that this is not a new topic. Homosexuality has been around for thousands of years, and the Word does have instruction on it. Our job is to read the Word and do what it says as we follow the Holy Spirit's guidance in how to minister. We cannot biblically define homosexuality as right behavior, but we can respond with compassion to those who are involved.

In the first chapter of Romans, it describes a reprobate mind becoming vain in imagination, having a heart darkened leading to vile affections, and changing the natural use of what a body is for into that which is against nature. In the beginning, "God created man in His own image, in the image of God created he him; male and female created he them." (Gen. 1:27, *KJV*). His original design was male and female, man and woman, husband and wife. His natural order was that each would have intentional desire for the opposite sex. Homosexuality is unnatural affection that goes against His natural order of creation. Satan brings deception in the mind as early as he possibly can to convince people they were born homosexual or in the wrong gendered body. He will begin very subtly at first until the thoughts become absolute torment. People quickly come to believe the lie that the only way *out* is to give *in* to the flesh.

There are several reasons why people are on the path of homosexuality or want to become transgender, and it varies person to person. They have often dealt with rejection, lust, some type of abuse in their past, an over-controlling parent, bullying, heavy influence from peers, or plain curiosity. Many live in a cloud of unhappiness and don't want to accept themselves for who God made them to be. The search to be loved and praised is never ending as they constantly seek validation and get caught up in the comparison game. They all have a story and we have a society that pushes agreement with gender confusion, causing many people to be swayed in that direction. Many believe they were born in the wrong body but God does not make mistakes. There is no fault or failure in Him, and everything He created is good according to the first chapter of Genesis. To say that God created the wrong gender can only come from someone who is tormented by their thoughts and feelings not matching up with what they see in the mirror.

Identity has always been under attack. Knowing who you are in Christ is one of the most important things you can find out in your life. When tormenting thoughts are pelting a teenager's mind that they were born the wrong way, or that they are attracted to the same sex, their identity is being attacked. Those thoughts from hell need to be resisted. The devil is "a liar and the father of it" (John 8:44). He's subtle, sneaky, and manipulative. We have to "be sober, be vigilant; because your adversary the devil, as a roaring lion, walketh about, seeking whom he may devour" (1 Ptr. 5:8, *KJV*). He needs to be resisted and not given in to. You are to "submit yourselves therefore to God. Resist the devil and he will flee from you" (Jas. 4:7, *KJV*). The more revelation your teenagers receive on who they are in Christ, the more confident they will be in submitting themselves to God and resisting the lies from satan. Demonic spirits are no match for God's blood and power.

The good news is that Jesus has provided freedom for those who will reach out and take hold. He bought us back, defeated satan, and redeemed us. "In whom we have redemption through his blood, the forgiveness of sins, according to the riches of his grace..." (Eph. 1:7, *KJV*). He has already given us everything we will ever need to walk in victory, wisdom, and power. Coming back to the original design of what God created is available immediately for anyone who wants it. Change is possible! If people want something bad enough, they will go after it. Freedom in Christ is what we cannot live without on this earth. He provides the way out, takes the heavy load off our backs, and brings us home in Him. By "...rightly dividing the word of truth" (2 Tim. 2:15, *KJV*), it will bring clarity to help make people free. Speak the Name of Jesus into the situation. The Name of Jesus has the power in it to unleash freedom and take care of the tormenting spirits from hell that put people in bondage.

Have your kids focus on the word of truth that God made them righteous and in right standing before Him. Show your teenagers scripture from the Bible of what God says about homosexuality and by "speaking the truth in love (we will) grow up into Him in all things" (Eph. 4:15, *KJV*). The more truth teenagers know and believe, the more spiritual ammo against the enemy they will know how to use. If they don't know how to fight, if they don't realize what's happening in the middle of an attack, they will yield to the wrong spirit and open the door for the enemy to come in. Jesus paid a high price for our path to freedom at the cross and has provided the power to overcome the sinful desires of the flesh. Victory is 100% attainable and anyone can receive it. "For whatsoever is born of God overcometh the world: and this is the victory that overcometh the world, our faith" (1 John 5:4, *KJV*).

Help the kids who come to your youth group that identify as LGBTQ. Help them by treating them just like how you treat everyone else—with kindness, with respect, and with the God kind of love (1 Cor. 13:1-8). There is no respect of persons with God, and neither should we have any. Don't avoid transgender or homosexual teenagers and don't shame them. Talk to them like any other human being. I remember asking one of my youth girls what was going on in her mind. She would come with a boyfriend one week and a girlfriend the next. In tears, she told me she was so confused and didn't know who she was. The affirmation of her peers towards the radical choices she was making gave her the attention she craved and made her feel confident. Yet on the inside she was crying out for truth. Being lesbian, gay, bisexual, or transgender isn't our created purpose or design, and the Father wants to draw these people towards Him like He draws all of us. He is the one that can heal the wounds of the past and bring them into peace (Psa. 147:3).

I find that many LGBTQ people often mention their feelings as a reason why they are living the way they do. They believe that if they are in the wrong about living their life as a transgender or homosexual, then why do their feelings and desires have such a strong pull on them? It's a valid question. Feelings are real. We as humans have been given emotions by God for a reason. The danger zone is when you let those feelings begin to lead you instead of help you. They are not to take the lead because they are so unreliable. Just imagine what this world would look like if everyone acted on what they felt and did what they wanted! It would be absolute chaos. Your spirit needs to be in the lead, and if your emotional realm (your flesh) tries to take that position, say, "Emotions, you line up with what the Word of God says right now, in the name of Jesus". Galatians 5:24 says those who belong to Christ Jesus have crucified the flesh with its passions and desires. When we walk in the Spirit, we won't fulfill the lust of our flesh (Gal. 5:16-17, *NKJV*). When, by the Spirit, we put to death the deeds of the flesh, we will live. The book of Romans is a great place to start when learning how to overcome fleshly desires and find freedom in Jesus.

Let the Father deal with your teenagers in their personal lives and choices they are making. It is the goodness of God that leads people to repentance (Rom. 2:4). You are not their Holy Spirit. This is an especially important truth. The second you start dictating what they should be doing, or how they need to get it together, you've missed it. You don't need to delve into where they are wrong and bring guilt and shame upon them. Your job is to open the Word to them and shepherd the group that you have been given charge over. There is a time for wise counsel, a time where they need to know truth and see it in the Bible, and a time where their eyes will be opened, but it will be God who will reveal to them what they need to do. Let the Father do the changing and the heavy lifting. You keep listening for exactly what He wants you to say, and when, or if, He wants you to say it.

When a teenager would purposely bring up the subject of their boyfriend or girlfriend and their lifestyle in front of the other kids at youth, I would get their attention and kindly pull them aside to let them know that in youth group we endeavor to talk about the things that honor the Lord (Col. 3:1-10). I saw it no different than not talking about the latest drinking party and how much alcohol was consumed, or who had sex with who on the weekend. None of this behavior needs to be magnified. All of your kids need to understand what is and is not honoring to the Lord. "Finally, brethren, whatever things are true, whatever things are noble, whatever things are just, whatever things are pure, whatever things are lovely, whatever things are of good report, if there is any virtue and if there is anything praiseworthy—meditate on these things (Phil. 4:8, *NKJV*). When you come together as a group for a few hours on a Wednesday night, it's to "...grow in the grace and knowledge of our Lord and Savior Jesus Christ" (2 Pet. 3:18, *NKJV*), to grow in relationship with God, and to find out who we are *in Him*.

When my teenagers would start talking about a kid at school who came out as gay, I would cut in on the conversation and ask who was bringing them to youth next week. I wanted them all. Every homosexual, bisexual, transgender person at their school, I wanted the ones on drugs to come, and the ones that were pregnant, or who had the abortion. Bring the wild partiers and the ones that smoke. I wanted every teenager who would dare to come to a Bible Study on a Wednesday night. Learning that you can have a personal relationship with the God who created you and loves you is for every person on this planet. Who did Jesus minister to when He traveled around teaching, preaching, and healing? Was it not the prostitutes, the sinners, the outcasts, the sick, and the broken? Get the spirit of religious thinking out of your group. Youth is not just for the good kids and the ones that rarely mess up. Half of my kids hadn't ever been to a church consistently before, if ever. Praise God that they were bold enough to show up!

Often, the other kids don't know how to handle being around someone living this lifestyle, and a large majority will stay away from even talking with them because they don't want to be labeled by their peers that they are LGBTQ as well. This is a classic case of the fear of man. High school is high school; teens will talk, make assumptions, and spread gossip. Encourage your kids to not let any pressure bother them. Show them the scriptures to stand on so they won't be swayed. One of my kids came to me and told me that they always felt the Holy Spirit nudging them to talk to this one teenager who professed to be gay. I encouraged them to yield to God's voice. Who better to reach the kids in their own high school but fellow peers. The Word tells us that "the harvest truly is plenteous; but the laborers are few" (Matt. 9:37, *KJV*).

There are certain boundary lines that will need to be set in place. We cannot endorse what the LGBTQ community is walking in, but they need ministered to as much as any other teenager in your group. I found that the homosexual teens who came to youth would always want to talk about their lifestyle and bring it up quite often in conversation. I would instead begin talking with them about how their relationship with God was going. Where are they at with Him? Their attention needs to be drawn off of themselves and their thought life. Always direct the conversation back around to talking about the Lord. Encourage them to not compare themselves with others (2 Cor. 10:12) and to spend less time scrolling on social media. Show them the truth if they are open to hearing it. Firmly stand in the place of agreeing to disagree when it comes to what they are acting upon. This doesn't mean you don't love them. Be settled and comfortable in where you are to biblically stand regarding this topic.

When LGBTQ people make the decision to walk away from their lifestyle, the subsequent sin struggle is no surprise to God. The enemy isn't about to give up his territory so easily and will provide plenty of opportunities for temptation and for falling back into old ways. The thoughts that homosexual and transgender people have are very real. There is a storm on the inside of them that does not go away easily. It's a fight through and through. The battlefield of the mind is where the warfare continues, but God said "the weapons of our warfare are not carnal, but mighty through God to the pulling down of strongholds" (2 Cor. 10:4, *KJV*). They have to fight those fleshly thoughts with words. The second an ungodly thought shows up in their mind, it needs to be resisted. For example, if the thought floats in their mind that they should look at porn, or grab a blade to cut themselves, or entice someone sexually of the same gender, immediately they can say out loud, "that's not my thought, I take that thought captive in the name of Jesus!" When it pops back in ten seconds later, say it again! And again. And again, until it's gone. As sinful thoughts are taken captive by the Blood of Jesus day after day, the struggle will become less and less. We overcome the devil's temptation by the blood of the Lamb, and by the *word* of our testimony (Rev. 12:11, *KJV*). Our testimony is about the victory we have in Jesus' Name and in Jesus' Blood!

The thoughts and longings of the flesh will probably not dissipate overnight, but it will happen as the desire to please God and to act on the Word becomes more important than the desire to please the flesh. Jesus loves homosexuals and transgender people very much; He died on the cross for them just like everyone else. "God commends His love toward us, in that, while we were yet sinners, Christ died for us" (Rom. 5:8, *KJV*). However, He is against the sinful nature of homosexuality and the perversion that goes along with it. When homosexual or transgender people take the step of obedience to walk away from that lifestyle, it's a hard decision for them to make. But as their focus holds fast to the reason why they are walking away and their mindset is to please God no matter how high the cost, they will discover greater strength and purpose in Jesus. Their renewed mind and thought life will begin to line up with the Word.

Both you and your teenagers most likely have friends or people in your lives who profess to be gay or transgender. The world will be forceful for you to agree and say the lifestyle is fine and that you're going to offend them or lose their friendship if you don't agree. This is where a line has been crossed. When you knowingly encourage their lifestyle to keep from offending them, you open the door wide up to the enemy's devices. You have placed the fear of offending them above what God has said, and this isn't right. As a Christian, you have to be spiritually alert. True friends who respect boundary lines that have been drawn will not require you to cross them. The one boundary line that should be crossed is the line a homosexual or transgender person steps over into their freedom in Christ.

The world will say that true acceptance requires condoning behavior, but to accept and to condone are two different things. Second Corinthians chapter 5 explains that God accepts everyone who comes to Him through Jesus while not condoning everything they do. Loving any person on this earth doesn't mean you agree with everything they do or believe. You are to believe the Lord Jesus Christ and stand by what He says, no matter how high the cost. We can be compassionate and not compromise what Jesus told us about what is right and wrong. Let's do it right.

Many, many people who have lived the homosexual or transgender lifestyle have come out of it, shared their stories, and have even dedicated their lives to helping others who are going through the same thing. They wanted to change and were set free through Jesus! Do the research and listen to the testimonies of people coming back to the Lord and how He transformed their lives. I heard one story of a man whose same sex attraction lifted after he forgave his childhood abuser. What a powerful testimony! Don't criticize the LGBTQ community. Pray for them! It's time for Christians to know how to minister to others that are struggling in this area. We cannot shy away from this topic; victory needs to be shared to encourage this generation of the freedom found in Christ!

Chapter 9

Suicide

Teenage suicide rates are off the charts. Guaranteed, you will have teenagers in your youth group who will be struggling with suicidal thoughts even when you don't think they are. The enemy is a liar and a killer and tells us so in John 10:10: "the thief does not come except to steal, and to kill, and to destroy" (*NKJV*). He is not about to relent in his tactics to steal life from anyone on this planet. The amount of pressure on today's teenagers to be everything they are not creates such torment in the mind, and they will hide how it is affecting them. You won't be able to see from the outside what is happening on their inside, but God sees (1 Sam. 16:7). When you fill the atmosphere with the life and truth of Jesus, it tears down the strongholds of the enemy. It's time to equip this generation with the sword of the Spirit and help them win in the battlefield of their mind. "For the weapons of our warfare are not carnal, but mighty through God to the pulling down of strong holds; casting down imaginations and every high thing that exalteth itself against the knowledge of God and bringing into captivity every thought to the obedience of Christ" (2 Cor. 10:4-5, *KJV*).

Each of your teenagers has a purpose and plan that God has designed for their lives. Their dreams and their destinies are planted on the inside of them as a seed waiting to be watered. The enemy's plan is to stop those dreams and purposes from ever coming to pass, so he starts early. If he can get them to believe that their lives don't matter and that everyone else around them is better off without them, he will. Thankfully, the power of God is stronger than the power of the enemy. When Jesus won at the cross, He took the keys of hell and death (Rev. 1:18), and gave us authority "over all the power of the enemy, and nothing shall by any means hurt you" (Luke 10:19, *KJV*). God needs His purpose carried out in the earth, and it's through people just like your teenagers.

It all goes back to the garden of Eden with the serpent's suggestion of "did God really say," in Genesis 3:1. Doubt was introduced, and deception took the lead as the forbidden fruit was eaten. One thought caused the wavering. One thought had Adam and Eve taking their eyes off of the Father who loved them and had them thinking and believing He was withholding something from them. One wrong thought in a person's mind like suicide being their answer is what it takes to start walking down a long, dark road.

The Father asks the question, "Who told you?" in Genesis chapter three. There is massive revelation to be gained here. We know we have thoughts coming at us all day long. Some are "fiery darts" from the evil one (Eph. 6:16), and others are thoughts of peace from God (John 14:27), but not everything that comes into your mind is you. That is one truth that every teenager in your youth group needs to know. God asked, "Who?" which means there is importance in distinguishing whose voice is doing the talking. There are many voices in the world, and hearing God's voice needs to be in the forefront instead being the afterthought. If it was the devil who told you something, that voice needs to be brought down immediately. The voice of God is what we are after.

As a man "...thinks in his heart, so is he" (Prov. 23:7, *KJV*) and "out of the abundance of your heart the mouth speaks" (Matt. 12:34, *KJV*). The Lord has designed us in such a way that the thoughts you allow to stay in your mind enter into your heart, and words come forth from your mouth affecting the direction you are heading. James 3:4-5 tells us that our tongue is the rudder of the ship that is directing our lives. What you think will direct what you believe, what you believe you will begin to speak, and what you speak is where you are going to go. "Death and life are in the power of the tongue" (Prov. 18:21, *KJV*). It all goes back to "bringing into captivity every thought to the obedience of Christ" as we are told to do in 2 Corinthians 10:5. The moment bad thoughts show up in your mind, you must bring them into captivity so they don't get rooted down deep and begin to infect your heart.

Youth pastors, pay attention to what I say right here: it is crucial that you teach your kids to WIN against their dark thoughts. Over sympathizing, showing pity, or watching them slowly sink into depression is dangerous. Show them how to stand and fight so they can win! Teach them how to "...take up the whole armor of God, that you may be able to withstand in the evil day, and having done all, to stand. Stand therefore..." (Eph. 6:13-14, *NKJV*). Your radar should go off the second you catch wind of anyone mentioning their life isn't worth anything. Teach your teenagers to treat those thoughts like somebody is trespassing on the wrong property and attack it immediately. Life is not a game. We cannot afford to play around, thinking that our thoughts and words don't matter. The Word tells us to "choose life" (Deut. 30:19). It's time to get serious about putting the devil under our feet.

You can't stop the thoughts from coming, but you can stop them from staying. Just because you are thinking certain thoughts doesn't mean they are the thoughts you have to entertain. If you ask your kids, they will probably tell you which thoughts they know they shouldn't be thinking. Thoughts of unworthiness, guilt, shame, condemnation, and anything dark and depressing, but many of them don't know they have the authority to make the thoughts leave. Give them some practical application in this area and show them how to do it. Say aloud, "I take these thoughts captive in the Name of Jesus" (2 Cor. 10:5). The second they show up again, we take them captive again, and we continue to do this until they are gone.

Suicidal thoughts are real. The devil will steal your joy and peace, destroy your thought life until it's in shreds, then plant a strategy in your mind to kill yourself until you follow through with it. The other part of John 10:10 says that Jesus came so "that we might have life, and that we might have it more abundantly" (*KJV*). Over and over throughout the Word, we are told to pick life, that He is the life and way, and that His life is overflowing with goodness. He died so we could live. "For God so loved the world that He gave His only begotten Son, that whoever believes in Him should not perish but have everlasting life" (John 3:16, *NKJV*). This generation, like so many others, needs to know they matter, that they have purpose, and that they are designed for life and relationship with Jesus Christ. When He is in their sights, thoughts of death evaporate.

Any time you speak words that Jesus said, it slashes the enemy and cuts him. When he shows up again, you cut him again. Use the Sword of the Spirit, which is the Word of God (Eph. 6:17) and speak His promises aloud. Satan cannot stand up against the Word of God; it is too powerful for him. Thank God we have His promises that are the weapons of our warfare. Praise Him for His help to win against the principalities and powers and rulers of the darkness of this world. The Blood of Jesus is far greater than any demonic attack coming your way. "And they overcame him by the blood of the Lamb, and by the word of their testimony" (Rev. 12:11, *KJV*).

Can you stop someone from taking their own life? Not really. You cannot will anyone to live. You cannot convince them in your own strength. Once they believe the deceptive thoughts that have been planted in their mind and decide it's not worthwhile to live, there's not a whole lot you can do in the natural because they will make it happen if they really want to. We do not have control over other people, and what they decide to do, but we can pray. We can bind those suicidal spirits coming against their mind and heart and intercede for them so they can receive inner strength from the Holy Spirit to resist the attack. Matthew 18:18 tells us that, "whatever you bind on earth will be bound in heaven and whatever you loose on earth will be loosed in heaven" (*NKJV*). We can speak the Word of truth to them from the Bible so that the veil can be lifted from their eyes. We can look to Him.

How will you know if one of your kids is struggling with suicidal thoughts? The Holy Ghost. You can make a guess in the natural and watch for outward signs like depression, cut marks, significant alcohol intake, or other things that suggest they are on a downward spiral, but truly only God knows. I have been surprised at certain kids over the years who I thought would never even think such thoughts, and they were the ones that I was on my way to the hospital for. They could be the most popular kid or the one that looks like they have it all together, but you just can't rely on what you see with your physical eyes or judge from the outside what might be going on in their mind. The Holy Spirit will alert you. Go inside and listen to what He is saying. He can warn you and show you things to come (John 16:13) if you pay attention.

Many kids dread going to school and think that if they can just keep their head down and not say anything they can make it through the day. My teenagers would tell me stories of the kinds of things that were said on a fairly regular basis just walking up and down the hallway. It makes a righteous anger come up on the inside of me towards the enemy for the games he plays. I told my kids to walk in those school doors with their head held high speaking the Name of Jesus! The spirit of fear needs to be dealt with because "God has not given us a spirit of fear but of power and of love and of a sound mind" (2 Tim. 1:7, *NKJV*). Your kids can know how to handle the pressure of what is coming at them when they know who they are in Christ and what they can say to combat the enemy's forces. Tell them to confess right words like, "I'm a child of God. God reigns in my school. God is my protector. I will not fear what anyone says to me. I forgive the people that have spoken words against me in the Name of Jesus."

Encourage your kids to watch out for each other at school. If they see someone say hateful things to another from across the room, that's the time to step in and stand up for that person. Teach them about the boldness they can receive from the Holy Spirit to walk strong and tall. "Have I not commanded you? Be strong and of good courage; do not be afraid, nor be dismayed: for the Lord your God is with you wherever you go" (Josh. 1:9, *NKJV*). Their reputation, or what classmates say about them, needs to not even be a factor when it comes to having each other's backs and helping each other out. You, as their youth pastor, cannot be there physically at the school to guide them or show them, but you can sure encourage them on a Wednesday night to be strong in the Lord and in the power of His might (Eph. 6:10).

The Bible will fill your teenagers up with right so it floods out the wrong. It reveals the lies of the enemy that say they aren't worth it and that life is always going to be this way. Those aren't their thoughts; those are lies from hell. Teach them that it's important what comes in their ears and their eyes. If there is garbage coming in from words, music, entertainment, and social media, then garbage will be coming out of their mouth. Likewise, if there is truth entering and good and pure thoughts, there won't be any garbage coming out of them to run things off track. Tell them what happens when they listen to dark and depressing music, when they crave the affirmation of other people, or yield to depressive spirits. It's a slow downhill process. None of this happens overnight.

A lot of the kids feel alone and begin to believe no one likes them or wants to be around them. They may not have a solid friend to spend time with. Or maybe they have plenty of "friends" around them but they still feel alone. They need to know they can ask God for a friend and that He can help them in every single area, big or small. James 4:2 tells us we have not because we ask not. I talked about the Lord being my best friend around them so they heard with their ears what God could be for them, too. So often, we think that we have to have these grandiose teachings and deep revelations for teenagers to receive, but it's very simple really. Jesus wants to be your best friend. He wants a fist bump. There's the lesson.

Make sure your teenagers know you are available to talk to, especially if they are struggling with suicidal thoughts. Ask the Lord to help you work on being more approachable if it isn't your strength. You might get called to the hospital to go see one of your kids who just swallowed a bunch of pills. A parent might be a wreck and have no clue how to respond, so they might ask you to take over and talk with their teen. You will have the grace to minister life into whomever you are around because of the Lord Jesus. You may not always know the right thing to say or how to handle certain situations, but just walk in step with the Holy Ghost and He will help you. He enables you and equips you with the right words at the right time.

We can go into all kinds of reasons why we think people choose to end their own life or when they started down that

93

track, or obsess over feelings of guilt for not talking with them or realizing they were struggling. Confusion, questioning, regret, and emptiness all flood in when we find out someone is gone. So many people are left in the dark over what happened and what they could have done. Friends, we cannot walk down the road of the past and receive the healing we need. We cannot live in regret or in the "should have" or "what if" danger zone. The world will say that God just needed another angel in heaven or it was just their time to go to make people feel better. This is simply not true; it is false comfort and false hope. We have to move forward and cling to the Lord and believe *His* truth.

Let me remind you of a promise in the Word from Isaiah 55:10-11. "For as the rain comes down, and the snow from heaven, and do not return there, but water the earth, and make it bring forth and bud...so shall My word be that goes forth from My mouth; it shall not return to Me void, but it shall accomplish what I please, and it shall prosper in the thing for which I sent it" (*NKJV*). Every promise of God coming out of a teenager's mouth works for them as much as anybody else. They need to know that when they speak words of life, the Lord Jesus Himself goes to work defending them, protecting them, and pulling them in to His stronghold of safety. The Word doesn't just work for pastors, it works for teenagers, too. Tell them this, because many kids get the idea that they aren't spiritual enough to receive from God, which is yet another lie from hell.

At the end of the day, it is up to each individual how they handle their own thought life. You can let the thoughts stay, or you can let the thoughts go. It's your choice. We get to bind the tormenting spirits of hell with the name of Jesus, and take authority over our soulish realm so that our mind, will, and emotions line up with what God says. We do not have to walk the road of defeat and think that everyone else is better off without us. Being lifted out of discouragement, depression, and despair is available right now. It's time to win in the battlefield of the mind.

~

Father, touch the minds and hearts of who is reading this today. Thank You for lifting the spirit of heaviness off of them as they choose to put on the "garment of praise" (Isa. 61:3). Be their shield, and heal their broken heart. Touch the wounds and the places that are broken, and pour in the oil of joy so the fog is lifted to see your sunshine. You have already delivered us from the power of darkness (Col. 1:13) and we choose walk in what You have already done. Holy Spirit, we thank you for being our comfort, in Jesus' Name.

Glory to God! He is one who sees and knows. He understands and He has been there, so release to Him what you have been holding onto. Give Him the broken pieces.

Chapter 10

How to Hear God

When I was seventeen, I got ahold of a teaching series by a wonderful Bible teacher. His messages on that CD album made a profound impact on my life that still remains with me today. The point that stood out was that if you could hear God then you have it made because He will never lead you astray. I wanted that. I didn't want to flounder around never knowing what God was going to do. I wanted to know His will for my life and be sure of it. I figured if all it took was learning how to hear His voice, I was all in! This revelation formed in me a burning desire to know God and be able to have Him closer than I ever thought possible.

I began to concentrate on figuring out the voice of the Lord and what He sounded like in my last couple years of high school. All I knew up until that point was that God for sure spoke through His Word, and the Bible was the one place you could go knowing it was Him. But where did you go when you opened it up? I did a lot of random opening and closing of my Bible in those days, not knowing what to look for or where to start. I also knew that the Holy Spirit was inside of me, and that He was my inner guide and witness, but how was I supposed to know what He sounded like? As I heard more teaching on the subject, I began to understand that He wasn't a feeling; He was an inner knowing.

When I began to adjust my inner ear to what God sounded like in my personal life, I got so excited when I heard Him, and grew confident in knowing when He spoke. John 10:27 tells us that His sheep hear His voice and follow Him. As I stepped into the role of youth pastor, I pressed my inner ears in to hear Him more than ever before because I found that when it came to the overall role of leading a youth group, I had to be communicating with the Holy Spirit constantly. He has a way to lead your group, but He is a gentleman—He won't butt in and He likes to be invited. Talk with Him about what He wants you to do and let Him in on all the decisions and choices you are faced with. It's called prayer! You might already be confident in hearing the voice of God and being led by the Spirit. For others who may be unsure, I'm going to walk you through some things that helped me know how to hear Him.

Picture the wings of a bird. Imagine one wing representing the written Word of God, and the other wing representing the Holy Spirit. You need both wings to fly straight, especially when it comes to being in the ministry. If you solely rely on being led by the Holy Spirit and don't get in the Word to back up the leading you are following, you will be flying in circles. If you just read and study the Bible but never listen and follow through on what path the Holy Spirit directs you to take, you will also be flying in circles. The Word and the Spirit are one; they go hand in hand. You must have both operating in your life simultaneously in order to make wise decisions and walk out the plan of God for your life.

The number one way the Lord speaks is through His Word, the Bible. "All scripture is given by inspiration of God, and is profitable for doctrine, for reproof, for correction, for instruction in righteousness: that the man of God may be perfect, thoroughly furnished unto all good works" (2 Tim. 3:16-17, *NKJV*). It's written for us, and it's in our language, praise the Lord! Everything in those 66 books comes from

God, and we need to learn how to properly discern that word of truth. Before your eyes are on His words, pray that you will hear from heaven and understand what He is saying. Keep it all in context. Who is talking and who are they talking to? Which side of the cross are they talking from? There was a major change that happened when Jesus died on our behalf. We live in a different covenant now (Heb. 8:7-13). You don't need to ask God to hang signs from the sky—just pick up your Bible and read what He has already written.

Remember the old radios where you turned the dial and tuned in on which station you wanted to listen to? I remember the slightest movement would either bring static or a clear voice on the other end. This is what beginning to hear the Lord is like. The problem is not that He isn't talking, He is! He talks all the time! His "station" has always got the latest updates, truth, and music from heaven. The solution is adjusting the dial on our end, and the dial is our ears. Not our physical ears on the side of our head, but our inner ears. God said in 1 John 2:20 that we have an "unction" from the Holy One, and we know all things. It is an inner knowing, something deep down in your heart where you just know something to be true. We must learn how to quiet ourselves down from the noise of the world to become familiar with His "unction".

What to look for when being led by the Holy Spirit is peace. The Word says in Isaiah 55:12 that we "shall go out with joy and be led forth with peace." If there are two different options in front of you and you don't know which one to pick, sit and think about one path first. Picture yourself heading that direction, going all in on that one decision, and then check inside to see if there's peace. The second path also gets some thought and an equal amount of time to see if it's something that God is involved in. When you sense the peace of God on one of those two choices, that is the one to move ahead on. If you are still drawing a blank and don't know which path to pick, a minister friend of mine told me to choose the direction that requires the greatest amount of faith. That piece of wisdom has led me on some of the greatest adventures with God to date.

My pastor taught me that if you ever get the, "I knew I shouldn't have done that," or the "I knew I *should* have done that," feeling, then that was probably God. He's like a green light on the inside. Something will just seem right to you or have a positive feeling in your spirit, and you will have a knowing that it's ok to step out and go ahead with something. Red lights come as well and you will just know something isn't right, and even if you start planning to head that direction, you have a yucky feeling inside. There will be no flow to a red light, and when you blow God off and push His red light out of the way, you will know it very quickly. Thank God He always brings us back on the right track when we miss it.

A check in your spirit is how you can describe when the Lord is trying to tell you something. It is like a nudging and an unction to pay attention. It may or may not be a definite no from God, but it's His warning to just stand still for a minute until you receive the go ahead from Him. These checks are not loud. He remains a still, small voice on the inside as Elijah described in 1 Kings 19:12, and it takes some discipline on our part to quiet our lives so we can hear Him. If we are too noisy, busy, and rushed, we won't even sense the check. When something happens and people ask, "Where was God?", that isn't the right question to ask. He was right there the whole time. He never leaves us or forsakes us (Deut. 31:6). The question to be asked is, "Where did I run past Him?"

We all know when we've missed it. It usually comes in the form of looking back at what happened whether it's that day, a few weeks ago, or even years ago. The would-haves, the could-haves, and the should-haves show up along with some potential regrets at the choices made. We seem to understand our lives better looking back, but we cannot be looking in the rearview mirror expecting to keep moving ahead. God needs us to get up and get back in the game. He will pick you up, dust you off, and set you on the right path when you are ready to let Him do so. "This one thing I do, forgetting those things which are behind, and reaching forth unto those things which are before, I press toward the mark for the prize of the high calling of God in Christ Jesus" (Phil. 3:13-14, *KJV*). Don't let the enemy torment you with how misled you were, how wrong your decisions turned out, or what pieces you'll be picking up off the floor when the dust settles. God doesn't want you treading that water and never getting anywhere. Thank Him for leading you on into the new things of Him.

No fleeces, my friend. No fleeces. If you remember the story of Gideon in Judges 6:36-40, he asked for a sign that if he was hearing God correctly, the ground would be dry in the morning and the fleece he had would be wet with dew. It happened. To make extra sure it was God, Gideon asked for a sign again, but this time it was for the fleece to be dry and the ground to be wet the next morning. It happened again. This was Old Covenant before the Holy Spirit came. We don't operate under this covenant anymore; we have a new one, and we have the inner witness Himself right on the inside of us. If you are asking God to have three people come tell you if you are supposed to be a youth pastor or help with a youth group before you make the move, this is the wrong approach. You are placing your trust in people and what you can see and hear with your physical eyes over God's leading. Learn to go inside because He will be nudging you from within. If someone comes to you and says that you are supposed to be in youth ministry, it should usually be a confirmation about what God has already been talking to you about.

There will be times when you hear absolutely nothing. You will check in with Him as you have learned to do, but this time for whatever reason, you are getting a big blank from Him. In these spots, I either assume that I just don't need to know, or that God has already told me something to do and I haven't done it yet. If God doesn't want you to see something, He isn't going to show you no matter how badly you want Him to. If you see too much, you will either run ahead of Him trying to make it happen in your own strength, or pull back in fear not knowing how to accomplish what He is asking. It's best if He shows you one step at a time. In the case of Him having already told you something to do, it's best to just go ahead and do it. Things won't move ahead until that step is completed, and you will be frustrated trying out fifteen other options trying to make things work. Be a hearer and a doer (Jas. 1:22-25).

Sometimes you'll know as you go. Faith requires action and movement because "faith by itself, if it does not have works, is dead" (Jas. 2:17, *NKJV*). Move forward with what you know to do as best you can and believe that He will come through with the next step when it's time. A sitting duck won't get very far. God has got to be able to work with something. You won't be able to see too far ahead most of the time, but isn't that what faith is about? We walk by faith, not by sight (2 Cor. 5:7), and we rely on the inner witness now. We trust when we can't see, we get out of the boat to walk on the water. We put everything we have left into God's hands and step aside to see Him work the miraculous. It's not about us. Simple faith in our Father with a willing and obedient heart will bring about the plan of God into the atmosphere of man. "If you are willing and obedient, you shall eat the good of the land" (Isa. 1:19, *NKJV*).

2 Corinthians 11:14 says "satan himself is transformed into an angel of light." He disguises himself to pull you off

your path. He will attempt to be the voice of God in your life, but generally overplays his hand. I can remember him going hard at me trying to persuade me to stay in Canada before I came to the States. He put in my mind one word and made it so big that it seemed like it was the Lord. This alternative plan would be easier because I wouldn't have to move to another country. Maybe this was God? It wasn't. There was no peace attached to it, it put me in emotional turmoil, and the pressure on me was so heavy. Things can look like Him and sound like Him but not be of Him. There will always be temptations of the like kind. Thank the Lord I got some wise counsel in the middle of that storm, and it was enough to pull me out of my fog so I could take a leap of faith where I couldn't see. God helps you where you're at. Never forget that. He always shows up and makes up for the light you don't have. "God is light, and in Him is no darkness at all" (1 John 1:5, *ESV*).

There are some things you will just know. God will drop some information in your spirit and nobody will be able to change your mind because you know it was Him. I can't explain how He does it, but it seems to be as real as any other fact in your life. Before I resigned from the ministry in Wyoming, I had started a Young Adults group, and within the first week or two of us meeting together, I just somehow knew I would have that group for one year. It was a knowing that I was very sure of, and I just decided I would enjoy each moment we had together as a group. God did not tell me *I* was going to be the one moving, and I'm glad He didn't. I probably would have gone ahead of Him making plans far too soon, or spending months wondering why and what He was up to. Sure enough, it was one year that I got to spend with those young adults, and I thanked God for showing me that one small detail so each moment with them was special.

God voice sounds a lot like you. If you are a no-nonsense type of person who makes strong and firm decisions, God will most likely be responding to you that way because that is how He has built you to operate. What you sound like in regular conversation to another person often sounds like the conversation that happens with Him in your spirit. He talks to me like how I talk to other people. He knows I respond well to a calm voice and a softer approach, so He usually speaks with me gently. I'm thankful for that. He is a personal Holy Spirit who is able to meet with each person exactly where they are at. He knows if you need a gentle nudge or a more serious talking to. "With the merciful You will show Yourself merciful; with a blameless man You will show Yourself blameless; with the pure You will show Yourself pure; and with the devious You will show Yourself shrewd" (Psa. 18:25-26, *NKJV*). All of the tones and words He uses fit each person perfectly so we know it's Him.

When you believe that you heard God on something and it comes to pass, it is so exciting! You will be so pumped that you were right on, and all the doubts that tried to attach themselves throughout the process will be dissolved in a moment. Breakthrough occurs, weight gets lifted, and your confidence level in hearing the Lord soars to new heights. You think to yourself that you will never doubt again, but then a bigger step of faith will come along right after and you will have to trust Him all over again. You will never really have God figured out 100%. Just when you think you know how He's going to do something, He comes through another way you didn't expect. It keeps life exciting, that's for sure!

It's always wisdom to ask God to show you scripture in the Word to back up what you believe you are hearing from Him. Things aren't always as clear as we would like (1 Cor. 13:12), so being able to put our physical eyes on what has already been written is a blessing from heaven. Ask the Lord to show you two or three scriptures along the lines of what you are hearing. "In the mouth of two or three witnesses shall every word shall be established" (2 Cor. 13:1, *KJV*). If the Word and what you believe you're hearing from the Spirit don't line up, you have missed it somewhere. What He says in His Word will coincide with what He says by the Spirit.

There is a time to ask for wisdom and advice from trusted people in your life but not everything you hear from God always has to be shared with them. Other voices have the potential to bring wavering and confusion to the table. If you have heard from the Lord on something, write it down, and stick with what He told you. The apostle Paul, after hearing from God, used wisdom and said that he immediately "conferred not with flesh and blood" (Gal. 1:16). It's often a good idea to not say anything more about it and not share it with the three closest people to you because they all have a lens they see through as well. Their viewpoint could have the potential to sidetrack you from God's original instruction. This obviously isn't their heart, but sometimes it is wise to keep things to yourself if you know you are easily swayed by what other people say. Especially if it's a life altering decision. If you need help, He will have the right people for you to talk to. If He wants you to keep it quiet, yield to Him, and don't say anything until He releases you to do so.

As you grow in your walk with the Lord and get to know His voice better, you will realize how much easier it is to recognize Him when He speaks. In my early years of putting out fleeces and doing a lot of guessing, I'm so glad He met me where I was at, but it was so much better when He helped me to turn inward instead of relying on what I saw with my physical eyes. Slowly but surely as I checked in with Him on different decisions and choices that needed to be made, I was able to gain confidence in who He was and how He responded to me. It's all about the inner man, the inner witness, and the inner voice of spirit connecting to Spirit. Your spirit is the real you, and "for as many as are led by the Spirit of God, they are the sons of God" as Paul described in Romans 8:14.

"Howbeit when he, the Spirit of truth, is come, he will guide you into all truth: for he shall not speak of himself; but whatsoever he shall hear, that shall he speak; and he will show you things to come" (John 16:13, *KJV*). When you have daily conversation with the Lord, He will let you in on things that you won't see coming. A potential problem with a teenager, a volunteer that isn't doing well, a parent issue, and even something really big that will happen on a particular youth night. He will show you how to operate more efficiently in specific areas of your youth group. He tells us to call to Him and He will answer and show us great and mighty things, we do not know (Jer. 33:3). His warnings, urgings, promptings, and checks keep the flow to ministry life going, because without Him, we can do nothing (John 15:5). He will lead you like the Great Shepherd that He is to green pastures and quiet waters. His direction and His plan for your youth group will be laid out in the still moments when you are quiet with Him. Where would we be without the Lord?

Most of this chapter has been focused on how to hear the inner witness on the inside, but God can use different avenues to speak to us. A passage of scripture in the Bible could stand out or jump off the page, His still small voice on the inside could be leading you, a message from a ministry podcast might come at just the right time, something your pastor said on Sunday morning could witness with you, or even a phrase somebody says could reveal the answer you need. Many times, I have been in a conversation with someone where they made a certain comment, and it was as if God Himself spoke right through them to me. Even the audible voice of God has been heard by some but keep the written Word of God and being led by the Spirit in the forefront. "Behold, I stand at the door and knock. If anyone hears My voice and opens the door, I will come in to him and dine with him, and he with Me" (Rev. 3:20, *NKJV*). He wants to talk with you! Keep pressing in to hear Him.

Now do I hear God perfectly? No. There have been plenty of things over the years that I have completely missed, and even this week I know I missed Him on something. Cut yourself some slack in the process of learning how to hear. God is not up there tallying how many things you get right and how many things you get wrong. There are areas in my life where I have become very confident in knowing the Lord's voice, and other areas in life where I'm still taking the tiniest of baby steps. The important thing is that you are moving towards Him, desiring to encounter His presence, and knowing Him more intimately than before, because when we draw near to Him, He draws near to us (Jas. 4:8). He will help you hear, don't worry.

Youth pastors need to know the voice of God and be led by Him just like every other Christian in this world. Hearing Him is vital to the success of discipling teenagers. Keep on pressing in and getting to know the Lord for yourself and help your kids in doing the same. Sure, you will miss it and won't always hear right, but you will get better and better in the clarity and the knowledge of what He sounds like. He won't ever lead you wrong. "Trust in the Lord with all your heart and lean not on your own understanding. In all your ways acknowledge Him and He shall direct your paths" (Prov. 3:5-6, *NKJV*).

As you adjust to turning inward and exercising your ears to hear in the spirit realm, you will begin to have the best of times with the Holy Spirit. He truly does become your best friend, your confidante, your counselor, the best teacher, and the greatest comfort you will ever know. "But the Comforter, the Holy Ghost, whom the Father will send in my name, he shall teach you all things, and bring all things to your remembrance, whatsoever I have said unto you" (John 14:26, *KJV*). Let's keep our ears open and our hearts soft to yield to our Father's voice.

Chapter 11

Prayer

In youth ministry, you will naturally gravitate toward the things God has gifted you to do. If you are an organized person, you will enjoy the planning aspect and do really well at coming up with events and administrating what needs to get accomplished. If you really like to study and teach, you will most likely spend more of your hours in the office studying and preparing messages. If you enjoy having fun and are the competitive type, you're going to be filling those water balloons and getting right in there with your teenagers at game time having a blast! However, there is one important thing that God needs all of us to do, and it is one of His top priorities especially in ministry. He needs us to pray.

Prayer is an essential ingredient to the will of God being accomplished not only in youth ministry but also in our own lives on this earth. It is the way God can move and bring His Kingdom into this realm. Jesus taught his disciples to pray, "Your kingdom come, Your will be done on earth as it is in heaven" (Matt. 6:10). I didn't realize how important this actually was until the season with my teenagers was up. Looking back now, I would have bumped up private prayer time quite a bit higher on my priority list, especially in my prayer over the kids and the ministry. I have watched the difference it makes on a day-to-day basis, and life is so much better when we incorporate prayer into it. When we pray, we lay down our own thoughts and desires to look to His and come into agreement with His Word, expecting answers and miracles to be done as He said He would do.

"Now this is the confidence that we have in Him, that if we ask anything according to His will, He hears us. And if we know that He hears us, whatever we ask, we know that we have the petitions that we have asked of Him" (1 John 5:14-15, *NKJV*). Prayer is not throwing up wishes toward heaven hoping that God will hear and answer them if we are good enough. When we waver in not knowing God's will, we will stay in that neutral zone and assume whatever happens next is what He ultimately wants. This is the wrong direction of thinking. His Word *is* His will. We must find what He said so we can stand on those promises. We take "the sword of the Spirit, which is the Word of God; praying always with all prayer and supplication in the Spirit" (Eph. 6:17-18, *NKJV*). Prayer combats the forces of darkness and brings the power of God into hard situations to turn them around.

Prayer is constant communion with the Father. It's relationship. It is an ever-flowing stream of sharing between spirit and Spirit. It is trusting His written words and believing that what He said He will do like He said in Mark 11:24: "Therefore I say unto you, what things soever ye desire, when ye pray, believe that ye receive them, and ye shall have them" (*KJV*). Believe that you receive *when you pray*. There are hundreds of verses on prayer in the Word. He waits for us to pray and be His hands and feet in the earth in this way. Keep asking, seeking, and knocking (Matt. 7:7). You can tell when someone is praying for you and what a blessing it is. It's not about getting together as many people as you can to pray so you can convince God to do something. He's already done it all at the cross. We need to get rid of our unbelief and trust the Father to do what He said He would do.

A friend of mine described prayer like going through a drive-thru. If you ask for a cheeseburger with fries and a coke, you expect to receive exactly that when you get to the window. If they hand you a pineapple, there's something wrong because that wasn't on the menu and it wasn't what you asked for. If you ask God for wisdom, believe you receive it! We are believers, so we believe! We take what God has said in the Bible and believe it, not looking to anything else but Him. "While we look not at the things which are seen, but at the things which are not seen: for the things which are seen are temporal; but the things which are not seen are eternal" (2 Cor. 4:18, *KJV*). It doesn't matter what it looks like in the natural realm. When we say scripture out of the *Word*, it is what God has already said and it's on His menu. Let's speak, believe, and receive what He said (2 Cor. 4:13).

Now, for the people that love to pray, this will not be difficult for you since you have already incorporated this into your private life. It probably has become second nature for you to go to the Father with your requests and the things going on in your youth group. For others, this is an area where you can ask God for help. He is not looking for eloquence or amount of time, He is looking at your heart. Lay before Him the burdens you have in ministry. Tell Him what's going on and ask Him what to do. "If any of you lacks wisdom, let him ask of God, who gives to all liberally and without reproach, and it will be given to him" (Jas. 1:5, *NKJV*). We need wisdom and guidance every single day, especially when it comes to ministering to our teenagers. We won't always know what to do, but He is always right there waiting for us to call upon Him. Heed His direction.

Prayer should play an important role in any youth group. Your teens will be listening to how you pray in front of everyone, but don't do all the praying—have them participate, too. Put your teens in small groups of two or three with a leader to practice praying out loud. Start by asking them to thank God for what's going right in their life. It may only be a sentence or two, but this will be a huge step for some of them. As their confidence level increases, they will feel better about praying in front of the whole group. Teach them to pray with expectation and help them match what they are saying with the promises already in the Bible. Show them how to "be anxious for nothing, but in everything by prayer and supplication, with thanksgiving, let your requests be made known to God; and the peace of God, which surpasses all understanding, will guard your hearts and minds through Christ Jesus" (Phil. 4:6-7, *NKJV*). Just keep showing them how to talk to God. Always thank whoever prayed and encourage the unsure ones of what a great job they did.

Pray when God brings one of your kids to mind throughout the day. Ask Him for help in working with a volunteer you don't see eye to eye with. Thank Him for the wisdom to share in an upcoming counseling session, or the knowledge needed to know how to proceed in a team meeting with leadership. Most of all, pray before each youth night and cut off enemy attacks before they even try to make an entrance. Pray that protection is provided, answers are available, and minds are renewed to see the light of God (Eph. 1:17-23). If we could see what happens in the spirit realm when we pray, I believe we would do it a whole lot more. There is power in prayer, in agreement, in thanksgiving, in requests, and in believing (Matt. 18:19). God told us to do it, so let's do it.

As we lay our desires before the throne and ask for the hand of God to be present in our teenagers' lives, the Father truly does help us on every side. He is *for* those teenagers coming out of bondage and wants them to win in every area of their lives. He equips us as pastors and leaders to shepherd His young flock and His heart of compassion is the answer to every teenager looking to belong and to be loved. As I prayed and believed God for the lives of my teenagers to be changed and the joy of the Lord to bubble up from within them, there was another avenue of prayer I often yielded to in my role as Youth pastor—praying in the Spirit.

When I was 17 years old, I was asked to pick my cousins up from their church in town one night and drive them home. I remember waiting in the car for their service to be done and decided to poke my head in the doors to see if they were close to finishing. As I quietly walked into the church and stood listening in the foyer, I heard the pastor in the sanctuary closing in prayer. He spoke in English for a few sentences, then switched over to another language I had not heard before. Back and forth he went from this language into regular English words, and I wondered what other language he knew. This happened for the next few minutes until he ended the prayer and everyone got up to leave. I was a little confused. As far as I knew, everyone in that congregation from our small town knew English, so why would he be speaking in another language?

As I drove my cousin's home that night, I asked them about it and they replied with, "Oh, that's speaking in tongues!" Just like it was your average, everyday sort of thing. They told me it was a special prayer language between a Christian and God, and when it happens in a public meeting, there is an interpretation so everyone knows what was said in the other language. I thought that was the coolest thing I had ever heard! I had no idea it even existed, and I was surprised I hadn't heard a thing about it especially growing up in church. I was very intrigued. Over the next few weeks, I thought often about this new prayer language and wondered if I could have it too.

There was a couple that helped at my youth group who I figured might know something about these tongues, so I pulled them aside on a youth night to ask them about it. They smiled and assured me they knew what it was. They asked me if I wanted to speak in tongues, and, of course, I said yes! It was something new I had not encountered, and there was a drawing and a pull to it that wouldn't leave me. They put their hands on my head and began to pray in English, asking God to baptize me in the Holy Spirit. I didn't know what that meant, but I could tell something happened on the inside of me. It's the same thing that happened in Acts 19:6: "And when Paul had laid hands on them, the Holy Spirit came upon them, and they spoke with tongues and prophesied" (*NKJV*). My tongue felt thick all the sudden, and I braced my inner self excited for the Holy Spirit to take me over and have this other language come out my mouth. But nothing happened. I drove home that night somewhat disappointed and wondered what more I was supposed to do.

Over the next three weeks, I thought and thought about why the language didn't come out my mouth. Finally, I couldn't take it anymore, and I sat on my bed one night to talk to the Lord about it. I remember saying, "God, I know they prayed for me, and I know it's in me, but I have no clue how to do it. Would you help me? I'm going to start praying in English, and You're just going to have to help me with the tongues part because I don't know what to do." As I began to pray in English, I thanked God for my parents, my family and friends, and for the many blessings that I had, and about two minutes in, halfway through a sentence, all of a sudden it happened! A rush of this heavenly language came flowing out of my innermost being! I was ecstatic!

It was surreal to me, and I truly didn't know what I had just come into, but I started to notice some things immediately. I could start praying in this language any time I wanted, stop when I wanted, switch to English when I wanted, and go back and forth between the two! It was so beautiful. The joy of the Lord exploded inside of me whenever I opened my mouth in this language. I realized I had been expecting the Holy Spirit to do it all for me when that couple prayed for me at youth group. What God needed was my voice to do the talking while He brought the words.

I knew barely anything about speaking in tongues, but that moment marked me. I could tell something changed in the spirit realm, and that I opened a floodgate of sorts—a gateway into something supernatural. Acts chapter 2 finally made sense to me, and I was so thrilled I could barely contain the excitement! I didn't know what I was saying, but I felt like I was finally fulfilled in prayer. So many times, my English words just didn't seem adequate enough, but when I switched to tongues, it seemed to make up for what I didn't know to pray.

Tongues under my breath throughout the day became my norm, and it brought me closer to God more than ever before, but I knew I lacked the teaching behind it. When I moved to Wyoming after my high school graduation, I was thrilled to find that my new pastor knew all about the Baptism of the Holy Spirit, and I finally got to learn and understand the biblical grounds behind it. Praying in the spirit, and even finding that I could sing in this unknown language, became my favorite thing to do.

Songs began to enter into my spirit from God, and deeper revelation of the scriptures came. Insight into situations became clearer, and it was like my inner man, my spirit on the inside, had a voice for the first time. Then I began to pray to interpret what I was saying to the Father like it refers to in 1 Corinthians 14:13: "Wherefore let him that speaketh in an unknown tongue pray that he may interpret" (*KJV*). Eventually, I started recognizing what I was saying in a few different ways. One of them was when I sat at my piano. I would sing in tongues for a minute, then switch over to English just like that pastor had done in his prayer at the church in my hometown years before. Out came the interpretation in English, and in a song! It was amazing. 1 Corinthians 14:15 was manifesting: "I will pray with the spirit, and I will pray with the understanding also: I will sing with the spirit, and I will sing with the understanding also" (*KJV*).

Tongues was my doorway into a realm I didn't know I needed. John 7:38 says, out of your belly shall flow "rivers of living water," and that is the best description for it. It's like you have a well of refreshing water on the inside, and your tongue is the bucket that draws it out. You get charged up, edified, and strengthened in your spirit (1 Cor. 14:4, *KJV*). It also became the release I was searching for in casting my cares upon the Lord. Great comfort was found while this language flowed. Right before Jesus went to heaven 2000 years ago, He told his disciples they would be baptized with the Holy Spirit not many days from His ascension (Acts 1:5) and it happened shortly after! Many people got this Holy Ghost baptism and received power to be witnesses for Him and this is available for anyone who would like to receive it today! All you have to do is ask.

The church as a whole has been quite divided over this topic for centuries. Many have absolutely not known how to handle the Baptism of the Holy Spirit. They have not properly taught it, or have tried their best to cover it up and explain it away. The devil does his best to keep people away from tongues because it's such a massive weapon against him. Very rarely have I come upon a church that both understands and knows how to steward it properly in a corporate setting. But they are out there! Quite simply put, if someone has a message in tongues in a public meeting, there must be an interpreter to speak in the known language immediately after so everyone understands what was said. God designed it to be orderly and not chaotic, and this is available for every church body. In your private life when it's just you and Jesus, you can pray in tongues all you want! There isn't a limit on your private prayer language. Paul said "I thank my God I speak with tongues more than you all" (1 Cor. 14:18, *KJV*). He was talking about his private prayer life.

I taught my youth kids about speaking in tongues so they knew enough to be prepared when they encountered it. Some of them received it and some weren't interested which was totally fine. Many people have resisted this topic over a negative circumstance or have had someone that tried to push it on them. Faith doesn't put pressure on people. This is not something to force feed fellow believers. Too many Christians have gone too far causing division over something that is supposed to be a blessing from God. This is simply a gift to be received. You can present the revelation and teaching, and just like anything else in the Word, people will decide for themselves if they want it or not.

In my youth group, I found that the more private time I spent praying in the spirit, the easier my messages would flow and come out to the kids. Insights, ideas, and concepts would enter to teach them a lot easier, and answers to questions they had would be more readily available in my spirit. When I wouldn't know how to pray for someone, I would yield to my unknown language and watch the Lord do something miraculous behind the scenes. Not that He can't do this without tongues, but this spiritual language carries something different that brings increase in multiple areas, especially in our faith. Jude 20 tells us that when we pray in the spirit, we build ourselves up on our most holy faith.

Even though I had praying in the spirit as a tool in my belt to reach teenagers, looking back now, I definitely could have put in a little more effort. Sure, praying in English and in tongues was something I did, but I didn't realize how crucial

117

prayer was for the will of God to be set forth. In this new season, the Lord has brought me into a place of immersion in all things prayer. So, in hindsight, I can see how it would have made things flow so much easier and stopped way more enemy attacks as I worked for the ministry in Wyoming. This realization has challenged me to press in more than I ever have before in this realm of prayer.

Both praying in English and praying in the spirit lays the groundwork for the Holy Spirit to move in the plans He has for your youth group. It cuts off enemy attacks and destroys them like the ocean tide overtaking a sand castle. It brings deliverance to the lives of teenagers and restores their mind, will, and emotions. Relief always came after every prayer prayed with my kids. Sometimes there were tears, but showing them how to release their worries and fears before God always brought the comfort they needed from the Holy Spirit. The Word tells us to "not be anxious about anything, but in everything by prayer and supplication with thanksgiving let your requests be made known to God. And the peace of God, which surpasses all understanding, will guard your hearts and your minds in Christ Jesus" (Phil. 4:6-7, *ESV*). What a privilege we have to pray—in our own language and in our heavenly language. What a gift from heaven to know that we have a God to call upon at any time of our day and night.

If prayer has made its way down your list, I encourage you to bring it back to the top because "the effectual fervent prayer of a righteous man availeth much" (Jas. 5:16, *KJV*). Line up what you prayed with how you talk about that same situation in everyday conversation. Make sure they match. If you prayed healing for one of your teenagers, thank God it's being done every time you think of it. Don't let doubt override what you spoke over them. Come to confidence in the Lord and in what He said He would do. Expect something good to happen! Just because you don't immediately see results in the natural doesn't mean God isn't working behind the scenes. Remember to "rejoice in hope, be patient in tribulation, be constant in prayer" as the Word tells us to do in Romans 12:12. Trust Him. Believe big. Expect Him to come through. He always does.

Chapter 12

Other Tips

My role as youth pastor was only a portion of the work I did at the church in Wyoming. I had a number of different things on my plate in that ministry, so I couldn't dedicate all my time to just helping teenagers. It was roughly a quarter of what I did on a regular basis. Because of this, Wednesday night youth group was the only night that I could regularly maintain for my teenagers. I would have liked to do retreats, mission trips, and more activity nights out of town, but lacked the time and number of volunteers to make it happen. Having said this, I won't be able to talk about helpful hints for extra youth group events, but I will share some other things I learned during my time with my teenagers.

~

When you look across the church fence to copy exactly what another youth group is doing, trying to get their results, you have missed it, my friend. The Holy Spirit wants freedom, creativity, movement, and a yielding to what His plan for *your* group will look like. He loves variety in everything and everyone, especially in a youth group atmosphere. He designed it that way on purpose! Does this mean you can't copy anything out there? No. There are plenty of materials and ideas that are excellent and a huge help when it comes down to the preparation of leading a youth group. It's a relief to know that you can type anything in a search bar and the internet will bring thousands of answers. However, always be in communion with the Lord on what He wants done specifically in *your* group. It might look different than anything you have seen so far.

Do your best to learn the names of your teenagers as quickly as possible. Write them down if you have trouble remembering.

Never judge how successful your group is based on the number of teenagers that come. This is a classic case of the devil trying to get in your head about what a failure you are. If you have just started a youth group, some nights you may not have anyone show up at all. No matter what the size of your youth group is, your goal is to reach the ones that are there, not get discouraged about the ones that aren't there. Focus on making disciples of the teenagers that are right in front of you. "Go therefore and make disciples of all the nations...teaching them to observe all things that I have commanded you..." (Matt. 28:19-20, *NKJV*). God will bring the increase as you remain faithful to do exactly as He says with the ones you have.

When the new freshmen come in, the older teens might try and pull rank and have them be at the end of a line, or go last for different activities just because they are the youngest. Put a stop to this whenever you see it. To that freshman, it can be quite a miserable year if this continues.

If a teenager stops coming to your youth group, let them go. It is tempting to go after them and ask them why they left in an attempt to get them to come back, but this can quickly consume your attention. It probably doesn't hurt to check up on them once or twice to make sure they are okay, but if they have decided to not come back, be okay with that. Keep your focus on the ones that you have.

In the beginning of this book, I mentioned having a joint youth event with other youth groups in my town. These worked out really well, especially in the summer months. We all met at a park and teamed up against each other for game time, then rotated who spoke at the end of the night. All the kids and leaders seemed to really enjoy the change of pace, and there were some great friendships and memories made during that time.

When your group is small, you can be a lot more flexible when it comes to game time and what you play or when planning small events on a weekend. It's easy to handle a handful of teenagers and quick to organize mini trips with a couple of phone calls and one or two vehicles. As the number of kids increases, you will have to be more organized and prepared. Permission slips will need to be made and signed by parents at the beginning of the year to ensure that they were ok with their teens' involvement with any youth group activities. More responsibility comes with having a bigger group, but embrace it fully and step up in this new area of growth! There are wonderful things ahead!

Because of the lack of volunteer power to do bigger weekend events, we were limited to things we could do around our town. We went to some college basketball games, and I had a few girls' nights at my house which went well. One of the churches in town brought in some pretty notable Christian artists throughout the year, so we did our best to incorporate those concerts into our schedule as well. A night booked at our local roller-skating arena brought in some new faces that had never attended a youth group before, and events outside of our church building were great tools for bringing in the lost.

Let your kids get involved in the planning. Have them come up with ideas for a few youth events instead of you doing all the work. They will rise to the occasion if you let them have some space to do it, and they truly do enjoy the challenge. It's also an opportunity to help them develop their gifts and talents for the Lord.

I wanted a way to connect with my teenagers more than just seeing them on a Wednesday night, so I asked the kids if they were cool with me coming to school and eating lunch with them. Surprisingly, they said yes! There is nothing worse than embarrassing your teenagers as they avoid eye contact with you in front of their friends at school. You are not their parent, but you are still an adult coming into their space. With the green light from them, I went to the principal to ask if it was okay, and permission came with some limitations. I was to sit with just my kids and wasn't allowed to "push religion" on anyone. Some people in the past had pushed that boundary and the school didn't want to get burned again. I honored what they asked of me, and one noon hour per week was spent at the school getting to know my kids better. I really enjoyed this time and got to have great one-on-one conversations with some of them. It's worth the time if you have it.

Taking the summers off is usually the standard practice of many youth groups across the country. Once school is out, youth groups also take their break. They might put on an event or two throughout the summer, but it is often a time of rest for leadership teams in ministry. I found pros and cons to this. I did enjoy the break in routine, but one day my kids begged me to have youth group continue through the summer. A lot of these kids don't have anything going on when school is out and are left to themselves all day. The year we continued Bible Study right through the summer, we maintained the same number of kids that came during the school year. Some nights different teens showed up because their youth groups weren't in session. I saw some great fruit come out of continuing the schedule, and it was a good way to keep kids out of trouble.

I always let my senior teens continue coming to youth group for their last summer after graduation. It's the end of a pretty big chapter for them, a special time to enjoy their last moments with their friends and their youth group family. Most of them stop coming automatically because they head off to college or begin working full-time. There will be some that stick around town and ask if they can keep coming in September. The answer to that question is no because it's time for them to move on and enjoy the next stage of becoming young adults.

Don't think that your youth group is going to fall apart without you there. They will be just fine; they can handle a week or two without you. Take a break. Take your vacation days. Go on a sabbatical if it's offered and available. You are always better when you come back, and it's a healthy thing to do. Everyone will have a better appreciation for each other, and you will come back refreshed by the Lord.

I usually didn't give my kids a heads up that I was going to be gone because I knew they might be tempted to not show up for someone else teaching. Teach your teenagers how to receive from the different anointings and giftings God has given other people.

Don't be deceived into thinking that your church kids aren't the ones struggling or having issues. Often, those are the ones that will hide it the most because of what people will think if they admit to making mistakes and having problems. The ones you think have plenty of issues can often be just fine, and the ones you think are doing great can be a wreck on the inside.

Encourage your leadership team to leave their phones alone while they are around the teenagers. Pictures are great and videos are fun, but anything personal or separate from that needs to be handled after the night is over and the kids have all gone home.

If you have a problem with anyone (teenagers, parents, volunteers, leadership, etc.), go to *them* first to discuss the issue and resolve what has been going on as quickly as possible. We get tempted to do this backwards and end up talking to other people about it before we go to the actual person we had the problem with. Be brave and have the conversation. It's incredibly important to maintaining unity in the ministry.

You are not their parent, so don't take on that role. End of story.

Set the standard for acceptable language the first day. Teenagers don't need to be swearing and talking filth. Teach them that when they enter the building it is a time to honor God and others around them. You don't have control over what comes out of their mouth, but you can sure set a boundary line on what is and is not acceptable. This doesn't have to be made into a big deal. I would often just give them a look from across the room if I heard them swearing or walk by and pull them aside for five seconds to say we don't do that here and then move right on to the next activity. Speak the truth in love. Major on what's right. Celebrate when they do the right thing and when they pick the right words.

You will probably have to bring up some rules on dress code and what is appropriate to wear. The girls will probably have more of an issue along this line. I didn't allow shirts that showed the belly or any cleavage. If they walked in with something on that wasn't great, I would just pull them aside for a second and ask if they had a sweater that they could put over it. Usually, one of their friends would have something for them if they didn't. Dress code can be somewhat of a gray area. Some youth pastors are stricter than others, but just be wise and discuss with your senior pastor what should be implemented along these lines. When I had the opportunity to talk with just the girls, I would tell them why dress was so important and how they needed to honor their bodies. It's also a respectful way to help out the guys since they are generally more visual and can struggle more in this area. Surprisingly, this was new information for a lot of the girls to hear.

There is a chance there will be some couples dating in your youth group. I was fine with hand holding and sitting beside each other, but anything physically beyond that, I considered unnecessary. No one enjoys being uncomfortable around a couple, and youth group is not a place to be inappropriate in front of peers. Keep an eye on couples that tend to wander off in the church building by themselves. They need to stay with the rest of the group.

Be a good listener. Teenagers need to be heard. They all have a story and they all have something that they have gone through. So many times, it's just waiting beneath the surface to be heard. Sometimes you need to stop talking and just listen to them tell you what happened to them. That's it.

Make sure your teenagers pray in the Name of Jesus. I only realized this revelation in my later years of high school, and the difference it made was massive. Our Father desires so much to do His will in our lives, and prayer in Jesus' Name is the key to unlock that door. John 16:23 tells us this: "And in that day you will ask Me nothing. Most assuredly, I say to you, whatever you ask the Father in My name He will give you" (*NKJV*).

God has gifted many people with musical talents for His glory, and we need to give our teenagers a place to exercise those gifts in our youth groups. Many don't even know it's in them until it is brought out into the light and encouraged. You might have a teenager or two that knows how to play an instrument, so have them play during the worship time if they can. It's not about how good they are; it's about learning how to praise and worship our King! This could also be preparation for their future. They may eventually be on the worship team in the main service, and it is a privilege to help train them in this area.

Your teenagers will be watching you as you worship, and they will follow your lead. You may have zero musical ability, and that is totally ok, but you do have a voice, and the Lord desires everyone's praise. If you are excited, your kids will get excited! If you don't show much interest in this area, they certainly won't. At least that's what I found.

Play music off your phone or on a bigger screen with lyrics so everyone can sing along. Have some upbeat praise music to listen to as well as slower worship songs. Get the kids used to hearing Christian music and be informed yourself about the worship bands and Christian music groups available. Ask them to bring some recommendations for praise and worship time.

Many of the playlists teenagers listen to don't honor God in any way, shape, or form. If it's catchy, or if it's the latest song everyone else is listening to, they will probably know it as well, thanks to social media and other forms of entertainment. Take ten minutes out of worship or Bible Study time, print out the lyrics to the latest popular song, and show them what they are actually saying. Listening to a depressing song will get them more depressed. "Death and life are in the power of the tongue" (Prov. 18:21, *KJV*).

Teach your kids about praise and worship and how it will "silence the enemy and the avenger" (Ps. 8:2, *NKJV*). Give some personal examples of how you have praised your way through a dark situation. When we put on "the garment of praise for the spirit of heaviness" (Isa. 61:3, *KJV*), it gives God great glory, and He takes our heavy burdens and brings us into His rest.

Cell phones weren't a huge deal. The only time we ever had to tell the kids to put them away was during Bible Study time. A simple reminder of putting them on silent while we looked into the Word was usually enough. At times we would have a group that found it tempting to look at their phones, so we grabbed a bucket and had everyone drop their phone in before we began. Most of the time it works well to just ask them to be respectful and not look at them. Again, don't make a big deal out of it. Just keep moving forward with what you have going, and if a teenager can't seem to follow what you have asked, try not to embarrass them in front of everyone. Usually while I was teaching, I would just walk back to whatever kid was being disruptive and stand by them for ten seconds while I taught, and they caught on pretty quickly. I would even hold out my hand for their phone while I spoke and take it back up to the front with me while continuing the lesson. Minimize those distractions as much as possible, and try not to stop everything and make it a huge issue.

Even though everyone already has the Bible on their phone, it's still important to open a physical Bible and know how to look up scripture. This will also eliminate the temptation of looking at texts and notifications during Bible Study. A few teens would bring their Bibles from home, but the majority didn't, so we had Bibles on hand for them. Take the first minute or two and have a good old fashioned "Find this scripture in the Bible" drill with some candy to throw them for a prize. If there is one teen that gets it first every time, it will quickly discourage the ones that don't know the Bible at all. I would have each teenager remain seated after they won so the others could have a chance at winning too. If the kids are quite unfamiliar with what to look up, encourage them to look in the table of contents and get them to find the book instead of chapter and verse. For many, this is the only time they will actually open a Bible, so show them some good basics that they will remember.

Most of the discipline that happened in our group meant having a youth leader sit beside the teenager that was being disruptive. It usually took care of the situation. We would have to pull kids aside and be firm with them as well. I relied a lot on the male leaders to deal with the teens that were being troublesome. I found my youth kids were always more well behaved when a man was present in the room. Men bring a needed authority which is God's design and I was so thankful when they handled the more difficult situations for me.

The adolescent age is full of kids trying new things, experimenting, and starting to make decisions for themselves. While they are in the midst of this stage, they will push boundaries. Some groups will do well in one area, and you will barely have to discipline. The next year the exact same thing will be a huge issue, and you will have to take away some privileges. We had a period of time where we only let one teenager go to the bathroom at a time so things wouldn't get rowdy. Keep your eyes open, and work together with your team leaders to have each other's backs in this area.

Cutting and self-harm will be something you see. The kids will hurt themselves on the outside, hoping it will distract them enough to stop the pain from happening on the inside. They will usually try to cover the scars and cut marks with their clothing, but you may catch a glimpse of them here and there. They may or may not tell you about it.

Some kids will probably lie to you. Not all of them, but be ready and listening to the Holy Spirit on what is true and what is not. As a teen would be telling me something that they supposedly did, or what their parents were ok with, I would hear God say, "Yes, that's true," or "No, that isn't true." Was it my job to correct them right then? Only if He led me that direction.

Have each parent's cell number and work phone if possible. You need their full names, which parent to call at what time, who's living with who, and the rotation of parental rights if needed.

I don't recall teaching my kids about the concept behind having a purity ring, but a few of them came to me privately showing me one they had bought, and told me they were waiting until marriage to have sex. This is huge, especially in this day and culture we live in. The ring is just a symbol, but it shows that they are being mindful of what it represents. Remember, don't just tell them to not have sex, be prepared to teach them the "why" of waiting, what a covenant means, and the blessing that they will experience when they save themselves for their future spouse.

When everyone is together for the Bible Study portion, I found that a circle of chairs for a small group of six to eight people worked well. Any bigger and things seem to get out of hand. The kids will start making faces at each other from across the circle and not pay attention to what you are sharing. Even having windows in the background can be distracting. Standing up or sitting on a stool to teach in front of them while they all faced me in rows seemed to work the best.

Be aware of the teenagers that are brand new to Jesus because you can do a lot of talking over their head without knowing it. They will be unfamiliar with Bible stories and Christian terminology, so keep an eye on who your audience is, especially when you teach.

During a youth night, announce to your kids that they are welcome to tell you if they have any games, concerts, or extra-curricular activities in which they are involved. You cannot make it to the majority of them, but even getting to one makes a difference. It shows that you care.

At the end of the night, say goodbye to as many kids as possible but keep an eye out for the ones that need prayer, an encouraging word, or a hug. Between you and your other leaders, this should be top priority.

If you are driving some teenagers home after youth group, make sure the last one you drop off is the same gender as you if possible (even if it's out of the way). It's just wise in the culture we have right now to be smart in these things.

When you make a mistake in private, apologize in private to that person. When you make a mistake publicly, apologize publicly to those people. Be humble enough to admit where you missed it. This helps your group understand you better and not put you on a pedestal in front of them. They will assume you are pretty close to perfect because you are their teacher and a few steps ahead of them. When you share that you messed up and apologize for it, they have so much grace for you that you didn't even know was there.

If you get hate mail, don't read it.

Your senior pastors may or may not want to have a weekly update on what's going on in your youth group, but this is something that you will need to discuss with them early on. Communication among leadership is what the devil really likes to attack in ministry, so it is extremely vital that you are in agreement with what they have asked of you, and that they know what is going on. You represent an important part in their ministry, so do your best to honor them in all that you put your hand to. Their trust in you means more than you know.

If you are single while youth pastoring, learn to trust and rely on your other team members, especially in your weaker areas. You won't have a spouse to watch your back or help you process, so your outlet will many times be people on staff at church. Help each other out where you don't see things, and keep communicating with them fairly regularly. Don't sit stewing at home for days over things that can be fixed or adjusted with a simple conversation.

You don't need a degree to minister to teenagers. University or Bible college time is valuable but not required. You need to be in the Word, listening to preaching and teaching, and spending time with the Lord on a regular basis, but don't let lack of schooling be something that holds you back from stepping into your calling. If God calls you, He equips you. Hands-on training was the best opportunity to learn I ever received, and I wouldn't trade it for anything. Being thrown into the deep end forces you to learn quite quickly, but it's effective, doable, and 100% worth it.

Chapter 13

Transition Time

Times of transition are never easy. There are minor adjustments made throughout the years with different kids and leaders coming in and out of your youth group, but yielding yourself to the new changes that come means everything. Change is often not looked forward to, but it is the one thing in this world that remains constant. The more transitions made, the better you will be able to adapt and handle them with ease. Get used to being flexible and open and realize that you don't need to be in control of everything. God will be growing and stretching you, but it's all in preparation for the next step He has ahead for you. First Thessalonians 5:16 tells us to rejoice evermore! Have joy through it all and learn from the Holy Spirit what He wants you to understand.

Each new group of kids that comes in is entirely different from the previous year. Some years you will have really challenging personalities that will make things difficult. Other years will be easy and the kids that come are great! Enjoy those fun and easy times as well as the more difficult years because they seem to ebb and flow. Watch that you don't get too frustrated and start to complain about the new kids if you are having problems with them. You are there for a purpose, and your job is to pray for them and shepherd them no matter who they are or what they act like. Find the joy of the Lord in every circumstance and in every teenager because the joy of the Lord is your strength (Neh. 8:10). Do a lot of praying for each group of kids as they transition into the group, no matter how easy or challenging it may be. God loves each one so much and you need to reflect His love onto them.

The first youth night of the new school year is always exciting! Every September, the new group of kids would burst in through the doors of the church. Sometimes I knew who would be coming, but most of the time it would be a surprise who showed up. Make sure that on the first day you speak to every new kid and do your best to remember their name. Ask them about their family or what type of sport they play. Get the conversation going. Some kids you will only see once and they never come back for whatever reason, so make the most of the few hours you have with them. Have fun with them and try to engage them in the activities, but be mindful of what they are like—some can be overwhelmed, so play it by ear with how much attention is directed their way. Be intentional, look each teenager in the eye, and thank them for coming when it's time to leave.

I found that each new volunteer that transitioned in would change the atmosphere of the group a bit, but as the kids got used to them being around, they eventually warmed up and accepted them as a part of the group. I would always give my kids a heads up on who the next volunteer was and emphasized the fact that they would be different than me. Your kids will tend to be protective of you and the group; they will take your side in a heartbeat because you have been with them longer, so encourage them to welcome the volunteer along with you. They will be watching the new leader and how you interact with them. Some of your kids will come and tell you what they dislike of whichever leader has entered the picture. Never side with them or create division over what they share with you. We are not unaware of the enemy's plan to divide (2 Cor. 2:11), so you need to stop them mid-sentence into their negative comments and ask them what they like about the new leader instead. Encourage them to give the volunteer a chance. You should be an example "...in word, in conduct, in love, in spirit, in faith, in purity" (1 Tim. 4:12, *NKJV*). If you show that you are in favor of the new volunteer, the kids will follow your example.

Depending on the ministry you are involved with, you may or may not have a say in who is coming in to volunteer. Regardless of this, you need to make the new leader feel welcome and at home as they transition into the group. Introduce them to everyone, and give them a place and a part in what you are doing. Depending on how much control you like to have, this could be easy or difficult for you. You will need to give them opportunities to get involved in different areas as you find out their strengths and weaknesses. Make sure you don't hog all the work; the new leader is there to help and to learn, too. Be okay with letting them take some of your duties. Who knows, they may even be your replacement someday.

Keep communication lines open with your senior pastors on how any transition is going. They may or may not want a lot of information, but it's important to share how well it is going or if you need help with handling it better. Your pastors will most likely have more years of experience, so ask them for any wisdom or practical advice they have. There could be someone who joins your team that is just not a great fit, and this will certainly happen sometime in the years you pastor. What you are experiencing needs to be shared with your senior leaders, and regardless of their direction in this area, be in submission under them as you navigate this new chapter. The Word tells us to do this in Hebrews 13:17. I like reading it in the Amplified version, which says to, "obey your (spiritual) leaders and submit to them (recognizing their authority over you), for they are keeping watch over your souls and continually guarding your spiritual welfare as those who will give an account (of their stewardship of you). Let them do this with joy and not with grief and groans, for this would be of no benefit to you." Honor them in how they ask you to handle the new leaders and be willing to bend and be flexible. This adjustment time involves some shifting around, but you'll come through okay.

Transitions were not always easy for me; I got used to how I ran things a certain way and it was sometimes hard to no longer be in charge of an area. My administrative personality would be a little too dominant, and I had to watch how much I opened my mouth, and really lean on the Holy Spirit in places where I wanted more control. You won't always get what you want or have it your way. You will get frustrated with people and not understand reasons why things have to be the way they are, but God will help you through the challenging days. You will learn a lot as you work with and around other believers and the Bible commands us to live peaceably with all (Rom. 12:18). These transition times often bring the most growth, so rejoice and thank the Lord that through Him you are well able to come through it all.

If you are just transitioning to another role in the same ministry, it's a much smoother ride on the emotional roller coaster. Not having to say goodbye is nice. There are now simply different factors to consider. Chances are you will be handing over your spot to someone else, and you will need to let them take the wheel without you checking up on them 24/7 to see how they are doing. They will do things differently than you and micromanagement is never fun to be under, so let them figure out their job and make mistakes. It can be intimidating as a new person coming in if the person before them was really good at what they did. Filling someone else's position can be tough, especially if you are around them every day and they know how you used to run things. Encourage them when you can and celebrate any new ideas they implement. There will probably be a few months where they ask you questions on some things, but eventually that should taper off and both of you should be in the correct lanes doing what your new roles require. No hovering allowed. Focus on the new role that God has given you.

Leaving your role as youth pastor is a major change in ministry life that causes quite the ripple effect. I suppose the earlier years of transition with new leaders and kids coming in and out prepares you for your final departure. You have built and established relationships, grown with your kids, shared your life and heart with everyone, and your teenagers truly do become family. Now, it's time to say goodbye, let them go, and move on to the next place where God wants you to be. The good news is that God has a way of lifting that sorrow and grace off your life so that you are ready for what is next and you are okay with moving on. By the time your end date comes, you will be more than ready to go.

My last transition experience was somewhat of a surprise to me; I didn't realize I was training the latest leaders to be my replacement. During the year 2020-2021, I became quite restless and unsettled. What I did not realize was that the grace to be at that ministry was lifting and slowly but surely, the things that used to bring me great joy and fulfillment were no longer there. I would think to myself, "Nancy, what is wrong with you? You love what you do!" Wednesday night youth group was always a highlight of my week, but the days came where I would be standing and looking at all the kids talking, wondering why I was even there. My years of youth pastoring at that church were coming to a close, and God was slowly letting me know that my time was almost up.

A few months before I resigned, the Lord was quite clear in telling me that I would be starting a new chapter in my life. You need to be sure that you are hearing from Him if you find yourself in this position. In ministry, there are many opportunities that will come your way where you will want to give up and quit. Because of the amount of Word going out, the devil does not want you in any type of ministry role, so he will fight you on it. The temptation to leave will come up time and time again, but the Lord's voice needs to be louder than the devil's voice; don't listen to the lies of the enemy. I can't tell you the number of times I had to shut the enemy up on the thoughts he was feeding me to leave early. It takes faith to find your place, and it takes faith to stay. No matter how difficult things may get, stay in your position until God says otherwise and gives you the release to move on.

Be honorable and give your senior pastor enough of a heads up that he or she won't get your load dumped on them unexpectedly in addition to what they already have. Tell no one of your resignation until you have clearly communicated with them about your plans, and ask how the rest of your time should be played out at their ministry. This can be an intense, tear-filled conversation, but it's the most important one. The church congregation and your youth kids only need to know later. Privately take care of telling your teams that you are leaving and just be led in who you tell and when. Things can get quite difficult when you are in the middle of this phase. You have basically checked out in your mind, and there is a temptation to no longer be as diligent to see things through because you know you are leaving. Fight to finish your race well. Do your best to not burn any bridges and don't get in a rush. These days are bittersweet. Love the people, say thank you, and let them know how much you appreciate them.

Telling my kids I was resigning was not without tears. Of course, they asked me why I was leaving, and all I had to leave them with was that the Lord asked me to. Thankfully, they had almost a year with the new leaders so I wasn't leaving them without a shepherd, but boy, it was hard to say goodbye! When you are called to ministry, there will come times where you realize how much people really do mean to you, and how thankful to God you are for them. Taking my hands off the wheel and closing the door for the final time was okay. By the end, I was ready to leave and excited about the next chapter God had for me. I encouraged the kids to continue in the Word and keep going after the Lord with all of their hearts.

We don't always realize the curves and turns ahead on the roadway of life. To be honest, the majority of what my life has looked like has not matched anything I had previously thought it would turn out to be. Just when you start getting comfortable with something, the Lord will ask you to move and shift with Him. Hold His people close, but be willing to let them go the second He asks you to. The ministry that He gives you is not yours. The people, the building, the ideas, the teachings—they are all His, and He has simply asked you to steward it for a season. The test comes when He asks you to give it all up. Does *He* mean more to you than what you are doing *for* Him? If you never ministered or taught again on this earth, would He be enough for you? Always hold your relationship with God above what you do for Him. Afterall, it's out of that relationship that you are even in ministry to begin with.

Chapter 14

Your Life as a Youth Pastor

As a minister of the Gospel your life is on display. You live in a glass house, and are watched whether you think you are or not. Who you are at home should be who you are in front of people. You are an example to not only your teenagers, but to every person you are around and connected to, and this is not something to take lightly. When God calls you to the fivefold ministry, there is a certain weightiness and responsibility that comes with it, but the anointing to walk in your calling will also be there. God sees it all, and He equips you for the task at hand. Do everything in Him no matter who is watching. Remember, He is always for you and never against you.

Finding your place is so important. God has designed a specific plan and purpose for everyone on this planet (Jer. 29:11) and it's up to us to seek after Him and find out where we are supposed to be and what we are supposed to be doing. Your greatest fulfillment comes from being in that place and many people are miserable today because they are off the plan of God for their lives. As Christians, we are all called to minister to people in general, but the call to the fivefold is specific and you will know deep inside if that's where God wants you. If you are called to pastor, you won't be satisfied anywhere else. If you are *not* called to pastor and are trying to walk in that role, you will be very *un*satisfied. Things just won't work the way you want them to and you will be frustrated because the grace and anointing to do it won't be there. Find out where God has called you whether it's ministering to teenagers, running a business, or raising your kids! Find your spot and you will flourish.

Ministering to the Lord needs to come before ministering to the people. If there is one thing in this entire book that I would want you to remember, it's that. It becomes way too easy to think that time helping others, or time at church in your office, equals your personal time with the Lord. It does not. Isaiah 40:31 tells us that "they that wait upon the Lord shall renew their strength; they shall mount up with wings as eagles; they shall run, and not be weary; and they shall walk, and not faint." When you find yourself solely studying the Word to prepare your next message, that's your red flag. You need private, personal time with Jesus every day. Praise Him, glorify His name, take the time to verbally thank Him for what He has done in your life. Seek *first* the Kingdom of God and His righteousness (Matt. 6:33). Seek *Him*—not just what He can do for you. Guard and protect your time with Him. It is absolutely vital.

I remember the day I sat in my office staring out the window, wondering how I got to where I was. God had become my business partner. I would go before Him with my agenda and my lists. God, what do you want me to do here? What should I say to these people? Can I let this person serve in this area? What do you want me to teach tonight? All valid questions and all things I needed answers for, but it was all business. When was the last time I came to Him as Father? I found myself in a place of wondering how things had gotten this way, but the truth was, it hadn't happened overnight. Slowly, but surely, the business side of ministry had taken first place above Him, and I realized I needed to come back to my first love. If you find yourself in this place, take courage, He will help you get back on track. You are not the only one who has missed it in this area. It can happen to anyone. He loves you no matter what (Rom. 8:38-39). Don't forget that.

Ministry can get pretty demanding and has the potential to consume you if you let it. There will always be more to do, another person to call and pray for, and multiple problems to deal with on any given day. The Lord will help you find a balance, so you don't get burnt out. "He gives power to the weak, and to those who have no might He increases strength" (Isa. 40:29, *NKJV*). I was single the entire time I worked for the ministry in Wyoming, so I was able to freely give my time and serve without anyone at home waiting for me. However, single people are not exempt from the dangers of going overboard in their work. I really enjoyed what I did, but often added more to my plate than I should have. You can do too much, wear yourself down, and sadly be scraping the bottom of your barrel with nothing left to give. Busy does not always mean effective. The solution is quite simple. You must make it a priority to fill up daily in His presence and do exactly what He tells you to do—nothing more and nothing less. It's what Jesus did and we can too.

You will realize quite quickly that you can't just go do whatever you want. Well, you can, but you won't want to. The reality is that when you fall, it seems like you fall extra hard because you impact so many lives around you. James warns us of this, that "not many of you should become teachers in the church, for we who teach will be judged more strictly" (Jas. 3:1, *NLT*). The ripple effect is real. Likewise, when you increase, so many lives increase around you, and it is awesome to see people win and live in victory! Take a look at certain people in your own life. Has their example brought you closer to the Lord? Would you be where you are today without them? The choices you make affect many different lives. Count the cost, think beyond yourself, and take account of what you are doing. Does your life honor God?

When God calls you into the ministry, it is a precious thing. "For the gifts and the calling of God are irrevocable (for He does not withdraw what He has given, nor does He change His mind about those to whom He gives His grace or to whom He sends His call)" (Rom. 11:29, *AMP*). Keep in mind that you paint somewhat of a target on your back the second you say yes. Satan is out to steal, kill, and destroy, and you now are in God's armory handing out weapons to His people. You are a threat to the enemy's tactics when you teach people how to win battles and walk from their place of victory in Christ. Days of temptation will come when you will want to quit, take a step back, or perhaps even shut people out of your life. Circumstances you never saw coming will happen, but God will take you through. The Bible specifically tells us in Galatians 6:9 to "not be weary in well doing: for in due season we shall reap, if we faint not." Get back up, forgive, and love again. Let the Lord Jesus Christ be your shield. Resist the urge to throw in the towel and quit. Rejoice in the fact that you are a threat to darkness, and that you can do all things through Christ who strengthens you (Phil. 4:13).

Pastoring comes with many trials, challenges, and tough decisions that won't always please everyone. There will be hard conversations, confrontations, hurt feelings, unmet expectations, and miscommunication. There will be days where you won't want to go, you won't want to teach, and you won't want to prepare. Your spirit is always willing to help and minister, you just have to tell your flesh to agree and be faithful to what you have been called to do. We are warned of this in Matthew 26:41, which says, "Watch and pray, lest you enter into temptation. The spirit indeed is willing, but the flesh is weak." With any advance being made in the Kingdom of God, you can expect push back from the enemy. Resist the temptation to not have the conversation, to give into offense, to draw back, or to quit, for you are well able and well equipped by your Father to see things through.

Both criticism and compliments will start to come your way when you begin to lead. These can be behind your back or to your face. If they are negative remarks, do not let them bother you. If you let them in, you will slow yourself down, get a root of bitterness, and offense will eat away at you unless it is properly dealt with. "For where envying and strife is, there is confusion and every evil work" (Jas. 3:16, *KJV*). Water off a duck's back, my friend. Let those comments go. People will also say great things about you, which is really encouraging! Then comes the temptation of getting a big head. Stay in the middle of the road, and whenever you get a compliment, receive it like someone is handing you a bouquet. Say thank you, and hand that bouquet over to God. Give Him all the glory because He is the One working through you, and without Him we can do nothing (John 15:5, *NKJV*).

Prayer is like a red carpet rolling out before you. That red carpet is the will of God in your life and ministry that you get to walk out. When you pray, it puts forth the plans of God and clears the pathway for His will to be accomplished. Time in intercessory prayer cuts off so many plans and snares of the enemy. Praise God! We are told to "continue earnestly in prayer, being vigilant in it with thanksgiving" (Col. 4:2, *NKJV*). When you spend time on your own to honor the Lord and pray, many things will begin to play out the way they are intended. My pastor found that people either love to study the Word or they love to pray. They will often default to the one and not the other. I found that statement to be true as my tendency often leans toward prayer. Find that balance between both prayer and study of the Word.

Be wise about what you share and be cautious about with whom you share it. Not everyone can be trusted. You will have access to more information than just a regular congregation member, but not everyone needs to know what is going on behind the scenes in your church. In fact, very few people need to know anything. God will help you to know, and He will nudge you mid-conversation to not bring up a topic or to just keep quiet. These promptings are for your protection. You will learn how to keep things to yourself, and this is not a bad thing. This is wisdom. You aren't supposed to tell everyone everything (Prov. 21:23). God is trusting you with much. You won't often get to share with most people the things that happen to you personally in ministry, but be okay with that. Lean on the Holy Spirit and walk in self-control. The more the Lord trusts you, the better it will be.

Because I was single and lived ten hours away from my immediate family, I did not walk through the pressures of having a spouse and kids while working in ministry. I was flexible and able to be somewhere at a moment's notice without having to check in with anybody. I know this is an area that can be challenging in ministry. Your family will be involved with what you do to a certain extent, but you need to know your limits as well as theirs. Finding those boundary lines will be situation specific. What works for one family will look different in another, but the Holy Ghost will help you find the boundaries before you get into the thick of it. Stick to what He tells you and your family to do. It is wisdom to not allow church duties to consume you at your family's expense. Be present in your home; it's important to God.

I find that personal friendships shift and change as you grow closer to the Lord and walk in your calling. Grow together with the friends that are seeking the Lord as you are, and be willing to let other friends go that are heading down a different path. Surround yourself with people that are like-minded who love Jesus. Having other pastor friends outside your circle is so valuable. They will be able to give you a different perspective and also understand where you are coming from. When you are blessed with someone to help hold your hands up in battle, thank God for them (Ex. 17:12).

What a rarity it is to have a true friend that will pray for you and stay by you through thick and thin. We are not meant to go through this life alone. If you need a good friend, ask God for one.

Learn to tithe and give in addition to tithing, as instructed in Malachi 3:10. "Bring all the tithes into the storehouse, that there may be food in My house, and try Me now in this," 'says the Lord of hosts,' "if I will not open for you the windows of heaven, and pour out for you such blessing that there will not be room enough to receive it" (*NKJV*). Once you break the fear barrier and trust God to take care of your 90% when you give Him your 10%, you will never be the same. I personally went back and forth on this for a number of months before I went all in. Once I committed and made the quality decision that I was a tither, it was the easiest thing I ever did. Tithing needs to be done not only in your personal finances but also in your ministry. When people give, 10% of what comes into a church or ministry should flow out to "Honor the Lord with thy substance, and with the firstfruits of all thine increase; so shall thy barns be filled with plenty, and thy presses shall burst out with new wine" (Prov. 3:9-10, *NKJV*). Learn about the tithe, offerings, firstfruits, and alms.

From a practical standpoint, I found it a good policy to simply stay away from alcohol. Many will share a different stance and opinion on this topic. I knew if my teenagers ever saw me drink in public in any capacity, they would probably think that it's fine for them to drink, too. I personally just wanted to keep this door shut so I wouldn't have to be concerned about it. You follow what God wants you to do. He deals with each of us differently (Eph. 5:18), so be led by His voice, and if He asks you to give up a habit or change something you are doing, be willing to do it for Him.

Any personal social media accounts you have should honor the Lord in all of your pictures, videos, and posts. What you teach from the Word should match what you post on a regular basis, so you won't be sending a mixed message for the people looking at it. You are also a reflection of the ministry you are serving under, so do a good job of not only representing them, but also the Lord Jesus Christ. Sometimes the Lord will ask you to stay off of certain social media accounts so be willing to do this for Him if He asks. In regards to your teenagers, it's a good idea for them to find and follow you online instead of you friending them first. There will always be the ones that won't want anyone to know they are friends with their youth pastor, and that is totally okay. They're teenagers!

You have a faith tank that needs to be filled, and it's filled according to Romans 10:17: "Faith comes by hearing, and hearing by the Word of God" (*NKJV*). You will be pouring out to a lot of people every time you minister, and you need to be poured into yourself. You may not get to be in the main service listening to what your pastor is preaching, so it is important to watch the recorded version or listen to the message online after it's over. If there is a conference or worship event that you can attend that is outside of your own ministry, do it. Hearing the Word and being refreshed from the Lord through other ministries is a blessing from God. Divine connections, encouragement, and new ideas are brought to light in the corporate anointing at these events. Keep that tank filled so it won't run dry.

Spend some time praying in the spirit quite often (Jude 20). Insights, ideas, and concepts come when your prayer language is yielded to, and it will help you in absolutely every area of your life. When you don't know what to pray in English, let tongues take over instead, then ask the Lord for the interpretation of what you prayed. It can come in English words or other pictures and visions, but it's one way God helps you and shows you what to do. This gift of the spirit won't be in operation when we get to heaven; it is for this time right now. If the Baptism of the Holy Spirit is new to you, ask the Lord to reveal why He would want you to have it.

Just because you are in ministry does not mean you won't go through hard times. First Peter 4:12 warns us about this. "Beloved, do not think it strange concerning the fiery trial which is to try you, as though some strange thing happened to you" (*NKJV*). You are not exempt from the grief, loss, disappointment, or trials that come in this life. We know God brings us through these times, but people need to see that you are human. You will have serious and difficult seasons just like everybody else, so share later (if you can), the process of coming through those hard times with the Lord's comfort. If you paint a picture of perfection before them and give them the idea that nothing bad ever happens to you, it causes people to feel like failures when they experience their own negative circumstances. Just be real. Be authentic. Thankfully, when you come out of those difficulties, you are able to minister more effectively to others who may walk through those same circumstances. Continue to hold onto God with all you've got. He will remain your anchor in the storms of life. "I will say of the Lord, He is my refuge and my fortress: my God; in Him will I trust" (Psa. 91:2, *KJV*).

You are not someone else's Holy Spirit. It is not always your job to give advice or to figure out the solution to everyone else's problem. Let God do His job. You will, of course, be in a leadership position, and many will look to you for answers, but you cannot be every answer to every person. In fact, you will get yourself in trouble trying to be that answer for them. Sometimes, you just won't know the answer, or maybe you will, but God will have you remain quiet on the issue. Some of the best leaders are the most humble leaders who are "...quick to listen, slow to speak, and slow to get angry" (Jas. 1:19, *NLT*). Be open to what God has to say on the matter instead of sharing your own opinion. Most often, a sufficient answer is to be led.

The lone ranger is fine for the movies but not for the ministry. You cannot handle it all on your own. There is a reason why God describes all of us as a Body working together and not just one body part off on its own. "But now God has set the members, each one of them, in the body just as He pleased" (1 Cor. 12:18, *NKJV*). We need each other. I was always relieved I could go to my senior pastors for godly counsel and wisdom. Having leadership above you is a blessing. Proverbs 11:14 tells us there is safety in a multitude of counselors. They can keep an eye on you and usually have a good idea on how much you can handle or where adjustments need to be made. You can only see from the lens God gave you; others will help you see your blind spots and vice versa. Let go of control in wanting everything, and everyone, to do it your way. Other giftings and talents are waiting to be used and grown in other people. The will of God will be accomplished on this earth as we work together.

Above all, you need to laugh and have a good time! Ministry often gets too serious, too quickly. This chapter even got serious in a hurry, but you have to laugh. God does (Psa. 2:4)! There are some challenging circumstances you will walk through as you pastor so endeavor to think and talk about things that are going right when those times come. When the devil fires his best shot at you, just laugh at him! The joy of the Lord is your strength! Satan has nothing on you when you have Jesus by your side! There were many things I did not do right along the way, many tears shed, and circumstances I would have liked to see go better than they did, but you have got to hold onto Jesus with everything in you—He is so faithful. Keep your chin up and count it all joy as the Word says in James 1:2. What God looks for is a willing and obedient vessel (Isaiah 1:19) to work through and when we finish our race, we want to hear, "Well done, good and faithful servant: you were faithful over a few things, I will make you ruler over many things. Enter into the joy of your Lord" (Matt. 25:21, NKJV). Laugh and learn as you go. Give Him all you've got, and enjoy the ride! Fulfilling the ministry call on your life and serving Jesus Christ, the King of kings, is both a privilege and an honor. It is so incredibly rewarding and I wouldn't trade it for anything!

~

Each of these points have become so important to me in this last decade of ministry, and I know there will be many more to come. Your own experiences will differ from mine. Some things you can learn on paper, but most things you will learn as you walk them out. I was so thankful I had a hands-on approach and was thrown into the "deep end" of ministry right out of high school. I had to grow very quickly, but it was worth it. My prayer is that what I have learned and shared will be help for you as you grow in your own ministry and calling.

"And Jesus answered and said, Verily I say unto you, there is no man that hath left house, or brethren, or sisters, or father, or mother, or wife, or children, or lands, for my sake, and the gospel's, but he shall receive an hundredfold now in this time, houses, and brethren, and sisters, and mothers, and children, and lands, with persecutions; and in the world to come eternal life" (Mark 10:29-30, *KJV*).

Chapter 15

The Greatest Moments

There are some absolutely wonderful moments that come with being a youth pastor! It is such a reward to be called of God to walk in this role, and there are many times that you come away from a youth night so incredibly happy and fulfilled. Treasure these nights and bring them to remembrance in the more challenging times. When God puts the grace on you to be a youth pastor, there is no other place you will rather be, regardless of how well things are going. Take the time to thank God that He chose you to lead your teenagers, and that you are well able to come through in triumph. Give Him all the glory, all the honor, and all the praise.

The best moment you will ever have is leading a teenager to Jesus. To be the one that introduces them to the gift of salvation is both a privilege and an honor. When they finally call out to the Father and receive His forgiveness with tears pouring down their face, you cannot help but be filled with gratitude for what the Lord called you to do. It was always beautiful to watch when they came to Jesus all on their own at the right time, ready to receive. You may, or may not, get to be a part of your kids being born again during the time you have them, but just be patient and keep sowing the Word of God into their hearts. The Word always heals, always restores, always brings the life changing truth that is needed, and the harvest does come.

Water baptism was always an exciting day in my books! We would sometimes have a special baptism time with just the teenagers apart from the church congregation. Parents, relatives, and friends would come to support them, and it was a joy-filled time. I always had a deep thrill inside my spirit because of the freedom I knew it would bring. The miracle of the old man dying and the new man being raised up together with Jesus was awesome to watch. My teenagers would come up out of that water and you could almost tangibly feel the darkness fleeing. I enjoyed teaching them the benefits of baptism, beyond just saying, "This is what Jesus did, so that's what we do." There is so much more to it. You are marked by God, branded in a way, by His love and made free from attachments and sorrows of the soul. What a great moment to have a new start!

Another wonderful moment is when a teenager gets baptized in the Holy Spirit with the evidence of speaking in tongues. I personally received this prayer language when I was a teenager, so I became quite passionate early on about sharing this gift with the Body of Christ. I would teach the kids from the book of Acts what this personal prayer language to the Lord was all about and how to operate in it. Some wanted it, and some didn't. By educating them spiritually on what it all entailed, they gained understanding about the purpose for which God designed it. When their own personal prayer language came flowing out of their mouth, you could sense the freedom it brought. The real them—their spirit man on the inside—had a voice for the first time. Mysteries from God flowed from their innermost being, and a new chapter in their spiritual life began. Absolutely amazing.

I always enjoyed getting texts and calls from my teenagers when they experienced a moment of victory. Whether it was praying out loud for the first time or working up the courage to talk about God to one of their classmates, I loved hearing every detail of what they did and said. Usually, the call would come right after the moment happened, and they would be so excited they followed through on what God prompted them to do. Some of the best stories would come from a successful conversation they had with a parent or when they heard the Lord's voice for the first time and knew it was Him. Celebrate these moments with them and encourage them to step out on the water with Jesus again! When they put the Word of God into action and do what they have heard preached, it is truly a great moment that gives God all the glory.

Fulfilling moments came when my teenagers told me their lives were just better. You would visibly see their countenance become brighter, their eyes not be so full of sadness, or just sense more joy and contentment in them than before. They would share how their home life was more peaceful or how they let go of things that were a bad influence on them. Lives shifted into a better place because of Jesus. Some have mentioned that if they would not have had youth group to come to on Wednesday nights, their lives would have gone in a dark direction. Their one thread of hope was encountering the Lord on a youth night, and it was the only time of their week they felt safe in the few hours they were there. God changed so many lives around for the better, and He made those kids free as He loves to do.

Every Wednesday my kids came through the doors was a highlight for me. The bigger moments often get more attention, but those times come and go. It's the daily small moments all added together that make up some of the greatest chapters you will ever have in life. I enjoyed the laughter, the embarrassing stories, the fun games we played, watching the kids interact with each other, and the atmosphere of the room. It was the place I knew God wanted me to be. I got to grow right along with them, and I was very content in my role as their youth pastor. Wednesdays became one of my favorite days, and I will always remember my time with those kids as being one of the best seasons of my life.

Graduation is bittersweet. You have watched your teenagers grow physically and spiritually. You have prayed with them, cried with them, laughed with them, and they basically have become your own kids in a way. And now, you let them go. Your youth group will adjust to the new norm of not having the familiar seniors around while the new teens join in and become a part of the family. Your time with your grads is now complete, and God will be taking them in many different directions. They all have an assignment to fulfill from the Lord. You got to have a part in growing them up spiritually and showing them the Father's heart, so your assignment now will shift to prayer when the Holy Spirit brings them to your remembrance.

One last great moment is what I am discovering right now. Even though I'm not currently pastoring my own youth group and have entered into the traveling side of ministry, previous teenagers of mine reach out every so often to tell me where they are at and touch base. They share where God has taken them and what they have been going through, and it's awesome to hear their testimonies and see the fruit in their lives as they keep walking with God. I always appreciate those phone calls and texts and thank God for all of "my kids" no matter how far away they are.

I'm not sure if I can quite put into words the scope of God's plan in these last days. He is so big, and He has so much for us to do. Whether you feel adequately prepared to be a youth pastor or not, He needs you. "How then shall they call on Him in whom they have not believed? And how shall they believe in Him of whom they have not heard? And how shall they hear without a preacher? And how shall they preach unless they are sent? As it is written: How beautiful are the feet of those who preach the gospel of peace, who bring glad tidings of good things" (Rom. 10:14-15, *NKJV*). You might not be the sharpest pencil in the box, or the most talented and gifted person for the job, but God picks you! Yes, God wants you! Regardless of the fear of stepping into unknown places, you need to get out of the boat and start walking on the water anyway! Jesus will help you, and He is with you every step of the way. It's time.

Having had the privilege of ministering to teenagers for almost a decade is by far one of the greatest blessings from God I have ever had. They all made such an impact on my life, and I will be forever grateful for it. As I continue navigating this next season God has called me into, I often reflect back on the time I had with my kids. They taught me so much and I am honored that God trusted me to lead and shepherd them.

It is so rewarding and fulfilling to walk in the call God has placed upon your life. If you haven't found that place yet, take courage, it's waiting for you and the Holy Spirit will help you find it! The lives you reach along the way will be for the Kingdom, and many people will be touched by the Holy Spirit and changed by the Gospel of Jesus Christ. To God be the glory for the great things He has done!

~

Thank you, Father, for each one that reads these words You have given me. May it be a blessing to them. May it help them minister to their own group of teenagers. May You continually grow us all into the deeper places of You.

In Jesus' Name.

"The Lord bless you and keep you; the Lord make His face shine upon you and be gracious to you; the Lord lift up His countenance upon you, and give you peace" (Num. 6:24-26, *NKJV*).

Go time.

Testimonies

In addition to youth pastoring, I taught kids ages five through twelve on regular service nights at my church. The following testimonies come from a few of the teenagers and kids I've taught over the years.

~

I have looked up to Nancy as a mentor/role model for as long as I can remember. I have had the privilege to see her journey unfold from the beginning because my family has attended the church that she moved to my entire life. As an 18-year-old, to move to a whole new country takes an insane amount of courage and boldness that I pray for continuously. To see her walking in the fullness of what God had for her and was calling her into was so special and encouraging to a young girl. She truly was and still is a solid and Godly example of what it truly looks like to live your life for God. Nancy has had a huge impact on my life. I recently started serving on the kids team at my church and I am so grateful to have had such a great example to shape how I am now teaching and leading kids to know and have relationship with God.

J. M.

Psalm 23:6 says, "Surely goodness and mercy shall follow me all the days of my life, and I will dwell in the house of the Lord forever." God is always there even when we ignore Him. I would have never learned to hear and listen to my Holy Spirit if it wasn't for Nancy. She was always there to answer any question I had about God, scripture, or anything. I was baptized when I was 15. That year I was struggling with the enemy on depression, but youth group was a perfect place for me to go to feel the love and power of God. I got prayed for in youth group, I talked with friends and learned more about God and growing my faith with Him every day. One night I was fighting so hard with the enemy and I felt God just grab a hold of me, and I just cried and cried and thanked God and talked to Him. I always say, "in Jesus' Name, I tell the enemy to leave," and the enemy would go just like Nancy taught me. It worked every time! I thank the Lord every day for bringing such a God-loving, kind hearted person like Nancy into my life. She has always been there for me and loved me. When I felt I was losing faith, she would pray with me and talk to me for hours about God and it helped me with my faith and the love I have for the Lord so much. Youth group was such a safe space to go to for a lot of us. We all loved going every Wednesday night. It was always something I looked forward to every week.

H. L.

My faith began the moment I started going to youth group. I had always believed in God and gone to church every Sunday, but I didn't really retain any of it until the end of my seventh grade year when Nancy suggested that my brother and I go to youth group. I was on board and I didn't jump off the board after that. Nancy provided me with four of the greatest years of my life while growing my faith day in and day out. Through youth group, I met some of my very best friends and have made relationships with not only God, but people throughout my church that are inseparable. Although I cannot go to youth group anymore, I look back on those Wednesday nights and thank God that He presented me with that opportunity.

B. T.

Thinking back to my youth group days, the thing that stands out most to me is my youth pastor, Nancy, being there for me any time of any day—not just someone who would be there for a kid during youth time on Wednesday nights, but someone who was there at midnight on a weekday or 6:00 a.m. on a Saturday. It didn't matter [the time]; she was always there. I think back to the troubled times I had as a teen wanting to run from God, but Nancy was right there to guide me closer to Him. She taught me that God loved me regardless of my decisions, and that He forgave me for what I'd do. And for that, I'm grateful and pray my babies will have a youth pastor of their own that will show them and guide them to the unconditional and wonderful love God has for us like Nancy did for me.

T. B.

Youth was somewhere I could come where I could always have someone who I knew was there as a vent, mentor, or if I just wanted someone to talk to. It has left me with valuable lessons and memories that could never be replaced.

W. N.

I met Nancy during my sophomore year of high school, and going to youth group ultimately changed my life. I felt more connected spiritually than ever before, and the way she showed the love of Christ to students was rare to see. Her messages each week helped me feel seen, loved, and cared for by God. I can confidently say I wouldn't be in the place I am in my spiritual walk if it wasn't for that church. During such a formative time in my life, Nancy's consistency and intentionality helped me to see God's grace and purposeful movement in my life. She is now a mentor for me in my college years and is a steady, gentle hand that always helps redirect me to Christ. I am eternally grateful for her influence on my life.

F. A.

My family and I have gone to church for as long as I remember. Being young, I believed in the Lord, but there was still a lot that I didn't understand. Normal church services did not make total sense to me. My brother wanted to start going to youth group, so I joined him. Youth group helped me understand the pieces that I didn't understand before. The teachings in youth group helped me to grow my faith and made me who I am today.

B. T.

Nancy was one of my favorite youth pastors I ever had. She made others feel important and heard and the group she brought together made connections and friendships stronger. Youth group had a whole other meaning when she taught, showing the belief she had herself, and in others, making everyone feel included. The love I felt when I was there, and how accepting everyone was when I first went, made me feel like I belonged, and I had never been given that kind of acceptance. Nancy was such a wonderful, kind, outgoing, caring, and loving person. I am so thankful I got to experience that with her, and to be shown that there is hope and love in the world.

B. F.

My journey with the Lord started when I was eight years old. I loved church, and I learned that Jesus loved me much more than I ever thought. Then, somewhere in my life, something went very wrong. I stopped going to church, and I stopped talking to Jesus. I grew very sad and angry with life.

I didn't have anyone to fall back on. Well, I thought I didn't. I remember one teaching at church where we had to pretend that our pastor was Jesus, and we had to have full trust in him and it was shown with a trust fall. Many of us failed and stepped back and tried to catch ourselves. However, it taught us that we needed to have full trust in the Lord because he was going to catch us every time. I lost sight of that around 6th grade because I didn't think that I was needed in the world anymore and was in a very dark place. I went through 2 years of me being as far away from God as I have ever been not thinking He loved me or wanted me on earth. Then, one day, I decided to go to church again. I went, and Nancy told me to start coming to youth group. I started going here and there, but then Nancy and I had a one-on-one talk. She told me that the Lord loves me and that He had a plan for me. Not only did she tell me these things, but she showed me how to find the truth in the Bible. I once again was happy to go back to church and I wanted Jesus to be my best friend. I got baptized the same summer. Youth group meant the world to me, and it showed me that talking about the Lord is easy and should be done every day all the time. Nancy taught me how to forgive those around me, how to forgive myself, how to show people the path to the Lord, how to choose the right path, and most importantly she showed me how to love myself because the Lord has my name on the palm of his hand and He made me perfectly. Youth group kept me on the right track and pulled me out of a place I never want to even come close to. I wake up every morning with a smile on my face because I know that God has a plan for me. I encourage everyone to find their Nancy, someone to help show you what the Lord is and how you can have a relationship with him that is greater than any other relationship. He will fill the hole in your heart just like He filled mine.

P. H.

My time from when I was little (in kids' class) until youth group, Nancy made sure to always make it fun. I really liked how she would sing with us and we would sing together. Worship was by far my favorite. While in youth group, I was always very engaged because I knew I needed to listen. She made sure to not let the Word get twisted and gave the best advice.

S. S.

I walked into youth group one day after I had seen it on Instagram and it looked fun. The first day I was there and we opened the bible, I had no idea where to look for the verse they mentioned. No one laughed at me while I sat there clueless, the person next to me flipped my bible to the right page. The kindness and the laughs had me coming back. Everyone knew where I was Wednesday nights. I will forever be grateful for the opportunities, fun, and family youth group brought me.

K. G.

I've always struggled to have a connection with people within a church. Most of the time I felt judgement because I'd show up right as service was starting covered head to toe in dirt, sweat, blood, and cow poop. Guess I was just a cowboy kid surrounded by future doctors and lawyers. My family found a little church outside of town that looked like a barn. I was skeptical at first because I never really fit in with the people I went to church with. The moment I watched a man walk in with oil stained FR's and another with spurs on, I knew this was where I was meant to be. I started to become more invested and began to go to youth group where I would meet "the Canadian." Nancy welcomed me with open arms and no judgment along with everyone else there. For once I felt comfortable at church. Nancy would then teach me for the next 4 or so years about the grace of God. Of all the things she taught me, it would be patience that would deeply affect me. An old cowboy once told me "slow is fast." I knew this meant patience, but I felt there would be a deeper meaning. James 1:19-20 and Proverbs 3:5 are the two pieces of scripture I would hold onto to this day. This helped me realize that "slow is fast" means to be patient with not only people, but with God. Without someone like Nancy, I wouldn't be who I am today and wouldn't have learned about God. The kindest, most open-minded, and biggest hearted person I know, and I owe my learnings to her—the Canadian.

J.W.

My favorite memory with Nancy is when I was a little kid and my parents had just changed the visitation schedule. I was crying the entire time and Nancy was right there comforting me. Another favorite memory of mine would be when I sang "Jesus Loves Me" on stage and I didn't remember the words so Nancy sat with me on stage and sang with me.

T. L.

Youth group was a place to have fun with people your age and learn about God. Pastor Nancy helped me open up to Jesus and help me understand how good the Lord actually is. I miss youth today because it was fun to come to youth and learn about God, but it was also fun to interact with the other people.

S. L.

I started going to youth group with my friend. We weren't the best kids back then, but Nancy still took us under her wing. During my time there, my faith sprouted and I was able to clean myself up. I loved every minute I spent with that group. I will always be grateful for the experiences I had and all that I got to learn about my amazing Savior through my favorite youth pastor, Nancy.

K. R.

The dictionary will tell you that the phrase "service before self" means that professional duties take precedence over personal desires. I will tell you that this is true but extremely difficult to do. To truly perform service before self takes sacrifice; often the choices you make will be ones outside of your comfort zone. People who are able to do this and fully give have great integrity. One person in my life has shown me the true meaning of this phrase. My youth pastor, Nancy Klassen, has and always will be one of my greatest role models. I never in my life have seen anyone give themselves so fully to God. In Christianity, the belief is that to live fully you must follow God's plan instead of your own. It is one of the hardest things to do because everyone thinks they have their life figured out, and then God has a different plan. Nancy never worried about clothes, food, money, or gas in her car. She spread the word of The Gospel wherever she went, and she listened to God. She said He had a plan for her to leave without knowing where she was going, and she did exactly that. The people of the church were happy to support her, and now she has traveled all over America and settled down right where God needed her. She was never lost and never questioned her faith, fully giving service to the Lord over herself. This made her more whole than any plan for herself could have, and it inspired me completely. It amazes me how people can give so fully to the service of something and feel more whole than they would thinking of themselves. To serve the Lord with full faith, even when it takes you out of your comfort zone or is not a part of your personal plan, is what the phrase truly means to me. It is such a difficult thing to do because it takes the feeling of control away, but I have seen it done and hope to be able to do it for myself in the future.

K. L.

I was in a really tough time of my life and didn't know how to fix anything that was happening in my life, so I turned to God. I prayed for God to send me someone to help me heal. Sure enough, God answered my prayers. Doors opened and I was walking into a church I had never been to on a Wednesday night. I ended up having way more fun than I could have ever imagined. From the first time I met Nancy, I knew she was the person I had asked God to send me. She was the only one that listened to me and didn't tell me I was lying. She helped God heal me and brought God closer to me. I am so happy that I found Nancy because she became not only my youth pastor, but also my sister at heart and someone I can trust and look up to. So, I thank You, God, for sending me Nancy.

C. R.

170

www.ingramcontent.com/pod-product-compliance
Lightning Source LLC
LaVergne TN
LVHW052026080426
835513LV00018B/2191